DINNERS FOR BEGINNERS

Persephone Book N° 96
Published by Persephone Books Ltd 2011

First published by Hamish Hamilton in 1934
© The Estate of Rachel and Margaret Ryan
Illustrations © The Estate of Laurence Irving

Endpapers taken from 'Grapes' 1932, a printed linen designed
by Duncan Grant for Allan Walton Textiles; the yellow
colourway is used for the Persephone Books edition of
Good Things in England. In a private collection.

Prelim pages typeset in ITC Baskerville by
Keystroke, Wolverhampton

Printed and bound in Germany by
GGP Media GmbH, Poessneck on Munken Premium
(FSC approved)

9781903155868

Persephone Books Ltd
59 Lamb's Conduit Street
London WC1N 3NB
020 7242 9292

www.persephonebooks.co.uk

DINNERS FOR BEGINNERS

by

RACHEL AND MARGARET RYAN

✻✻✻✻✻✻✻

PERSEPHONE BOOKS
LONDON

TABLE OF CONTENTS

CHAPTER   PAGE

PREFACE –   –   –   –   –   –   7

INTRODUCTION –   –   –   –   –   9

NOTES –   –   –   –   –   –   15

I   UTENSILS AND STORES FOR THE SINGLE-HANDED KITCHEN –   –   –   –   19

II   GETTING DINNER READY IN TIME   –   33

III   SEVEN DINNERS FOR SPRING   –   –   42

IV   SEVEN DINNERS FOR SUMMER   –   –   104

V   SEVEN DINNERS FOR AUTUMN   –   –   168

VI   SEVEN DINNERS FOR WINTER   –   –   226

VII   IMPROMPTU MEALS –   –   –   –   285

SPECIAL RECIPE   –   –   –   –   296

TABLE OF DINNERS AND RECIPES –   –   297

INDEX –   –   –   –   –   –   301

PREFACE

WE have eaten and enjoyed every dinner in this book. Our wives have planned and cooked all the dinners. We say this at the risk of being reminded that what the husband says about the wife is not evidence. Miss out what we say if you like. But don't miss the dinners that follow. We have tried them, and we know.

A. P. R. and E. P. R.

INTRODUCTION

Tᴴɪs is a book for people who know nothing about cooking. At the same time it is intended for all those – whether they can cook or not – who appreciate good food and like to entertain their friends, but cannot afford to spend more than a strictly limited amount of money on housekeeping. There are a great many of us in this position to-day – young married people, single women living without servants, bachelors wavering between the ruinous Scylla of restaurant hospitality and the Charybdis of dry roast beef and rattling peas followed by highly glazed custard and tinned fruit salad, the whole gloomy ration concocted by some charwoman who may well be the kindest of the kind but has never had the time or opportunity to become a cunning cook.

It is for these people that the authors of this book have tried to write a cookery book that Exᴘʟᴀɪɴs Eᴠᴇʀʏᴛʜɪɴɢ. No knowledge is taken for granted. The beginner is not expected to know by the light of nature how to make gravy, sauces or pastry; she is told when the lid of a saucepan or fireproof dish ought to be on and when it should be off; she is advised what to ask for and how much to buy when she goes marketing; she is told how to serve food, how to keep plates and dishes warm and what food should look like when it is cooked. These are all very humble details, and yet information that may seem trifling to the experienced cook is often absolutely essential to the novice – for lack of it she may be brought to a complete standstill or embark on ruinous and wasteful experiments. So much of this essential information is missing in even the best of cookery books that the authors of this one swore to themselves that, though it might not be very big or at all grand, it must at least be thorough.

The book contains 109 recipes. These are all embodied in twenty-eight menus of dinners for four people at a total cost of 5/– (excluding dessert, cheese and coffee). Some of the menus are headed by notes explaining why particular dishes have been chosen. Recipes follow for every dish in the meal. Next, in every case, is a shopping list; armed with this, the cook-housekeeper-hostess can quickly do her shopping for each dinner. Finally, there is a time-table by the help of which, if she wishes, she can cook the meal herself, stage by stage.

The dinners have been divided into batches of seven for each season of the year, and each one takes advantage of some fruit or vegetable or meat that is cheap, good and in season at this time of year. Dishes have been planned to look attractive as well as to taste good. The menus are not arranged along strict dietetic lines, but each meal is arranged so that no one food substance shall overbalance the others. Every meal is 'self-contained' – there is no assumption that the cost can be lowered by using up 'left-overs' next day, for the authors believe that in a small household such economies are not really helpful. Husband and wife, or single householder may be in to dinner one day and out the next. Then why haunt them with the thought of the half-eaten joint that OUGHT to be eaten up?

In nearly every case except where fish replaces meat or bird as a first course, the meals chosen consist simply of two courses. If a hostess is serving her own dinner, her guests will not thank her for three or four courses, however succulent, that have to be whisked in and out through a door or a draughty serving hatch. She may urge 'Do leave it to me!' or 'We LOVE doing it ourselves!', but no male guest can sit with an easy conscience while his hostess posts to and fro at the back of his chair with a burden of dirty dishes. Long dinners mean extra washing up and extra devices for keeping each course hot while the one before is being eaten. Let the single-handed cook leave them to restaurants and big households which have resources to cope with them – hospitality of this sort in a small house or flat is merely fussy. As for pancakes, *soufflés* and savouries – delicious as they are – there are practically none in these menus. A good *soufflé*, omelette, pancake or savoury should be served the instant it is cooked. The hostess may think she can cook it quickly between courses. By all means let her try – but if she vanishes for ten minutes or so her guests may well feel that no dish can be exquisite enough to justify these wearisome intervals. Appetites that are fed too long on expectation and a muffled clatter from the kitchen will wilt at last, and the hostess may have the humiliation of rushing in with a perfect *soufflé* clasped to her bosom only to find her guests, like flowers too long unwatered, dull beyond hope of recovery.

The shopping lists in this book can only apply accurately to the time of writing and the districts in which the authors are in the habit of shopping. They have, however, compared notes with friends living in other centres, and have found that the variation in price of most essential foodstuffs is not very great. Big towns are cheaper shopping centres than villages. On the other hand, those who live in the country can make up for dearer meat and fish by growing their own vegetables and fruit. The authors have tried to deal faithfully with these lists and even small quantities of butter, sugar and milk are accounted for.

The time-tables have been very carefully checked over so that even a beginner, if she first reads over the recipes for a dinner carefully and then follows the time-table, should be able to produce a well-cooked meal without undue anxiety. Time is allowed for laying the table – an important item which many beginners forget. Readers are also reminded when to light the oven and put on water to boil and told when to start warming plates and dishes. There are notes at the end of every time-table on how to keep back a dinner if the guests are late. Naturally, these time-tables can only hold good where food is being cooked by the same method as that employed by the authors, who both happen to use a gas-cooker with automatic heat control.

In addition, there are chapters on kitchen utensils and stores for the small kitchen, getting dinner ready in time, and impromptu meals.

The authors do not claim that they have produced a book of exotic novelties. (The recipe on page 296 is an exception and only suggested as a portmanteau meal, the chief ingredients having themselves devoured all other food available in the district.) But every single dish in this book has been cooked and served by them, timed and tested in their own very ordinary kitchens and eaten with copious criticism by their husbands and friends. In the course of these trials, recipes taken from other sources have sometimes been altered sufficiently for the authors to feel justified in giving them a new name. The bulk of the recipes, however, have been taken from books and friends and newspapers or begged from friendly cooks. Many and many a one was thrown out, after trial, as being unsuitable for the kind of single-handed cookery which the authors had in mind; either it was too laborious or too expensive, or it could not be kept waiting in the kitchen without someone to look after it. Those that are left they most sincerely hope will please.

INTRODUCTION

As the beginner gains experience she may feel tempted to make experiments – to use fresh combinations of meat and vegetables or to embody a new fruit in a sweet which she has often cooked before. Some suggestions for possible experiments are made in the course of the recipes in the book. Even the most disastrous failure may teach the cook a lot. As for success, is there a sweeter moment in a cook's life than that when she answers an admiring query with: 'Yes, I invented that myself.'?

Cooking is endless fun. Once the beginner has lost the feelings of abject helplessness and indecision which it is the object of this book to put to flight, she will realise that one of the most necessary jobs in the world can also be one of the pleasantest, and will enjoy the exercise of her own skill as much as the continual health and pleasure which she provides for those around her.

NOTES

These are put under headings of butcher, dairy, greengrocer, etc., but there is also a heading in nearly every case, 'From Stock'. Under this appear quantities of food which are too small to be bought at a shop, but whose cost must, nevertheless, be reckoned if any fair idea of the whole expense of the dinner is to be given. Most of these items are things which would come under the main heading, *Grocer* – e.g., sugar, flour, gelatine. Parsley, which is only a penny a bunch, will last for several days, but where it is used in any quantity it is reckoned at $\frac{1}{2}$d. or half a bunch. Gelatine is reckoned at about 4 sheets to a penny, butter at 1/– a pound, flour at 1$\frac{1}{2}$d. a pound, and sugar at a penny for from four to six ounces. Salt and pepper are not reckoned, nor are any items used in small quantities costing less than a half-penny, although they appear on the shopping lists to remind the housewife that they will be needed.

TIME-TABLES

Italics are used for the actual cooking in the time-tables. Wherever it appears it should not be neglected. Other parts of the time-table may be fitted in in different ways according to individual preferences. Some people are quick, some are slow, but the actual cooking (granted the method is the same) always takes the same time.

The time-tables may seem rather long, for hardly any of them begin later than six o'clock for an eight o'clock dinner. Experience, however, will probably make it easy to shorten them, as in many cases their length is due to the fact that ample time has been allowed for quite easy kitchen operations. Time has also been sacrificed to avoid complications, i.e., where a cook with even a little experience would be able to carry on two operations at once, the time-table provides for these being done one after the other.

HERE ARE SOME MEASURES THAT WILL HELP YOU IF YOU HAVE NO SCALES OR PINT MEASURE AT HAND

Liquid.

One breakfastcup —Half a pint.
One teacup —Quarter of a pint (one gill).
One tumbler —Half a pint.
20 liquid ozs. —One pint.
20 tablespoons —One pint.

Solid.

One breakfastcupful flour —Half a pound.
One „ „ sugar —Three-quarters of a pound.
One „ „ rice —Ten ounces.
One „ „ crumbs —Quarter of a pound.
One heaped tablespoon flour —One ounce.
One level teaspoon sugar —Quarter of an ounce.
One „ tablespoon rice —One and a half ounces.
One „ „ butter or
fat —One ounce.

and

Sixteen ounces —One pound.
Four gills —One pint.
Two pints —One quart.

DINNERS FOR BEGINNERS

CHAPTER I

UTENSILS AND STORES FOR THE SINGLE-HANDED KITCHEN

A – UTENSILS

HERE is a list of the utensils that a beginner would do well to keep in her kitchen. Every one of these things should have a place of its own in which it is always kept; then you will always know where to turn for it when you are in a hurry. The stars mark things which are essential for cooking the dishes in this book.

*3 graduated aluminium saucepans, with lids.

*2 aluminium saucepans with lips for pouring. Have one double-lipped, as this makes it easier to pour with the left hand when you happen to be stirring with the right.

1 enamel lipped saucepan (this cooks more quickly, and is very cheap to buy, but not necessary).

*1 medium-size frying-pan. Two would be better. Buy really good ones, as the inferior kind are apt to get a dip or a hump in the middle and will then not fry evenly.

*1 oven roaster, with ventilator lid.

*2 or more, baking tins. Buy one round flat one for baking tarts or flans. These are very cheap.

*1 set of patty pans, for baking tartlets.

*1 flat baking sheet.

*1 double boiler, for cooking things which must not be allowed to boil.

*1 steamer – or steamer top with a graduated bottom which can fit over any of the aluminium saucepans.

*1 griller.

(All the above utensils can be cleaned with special scouring material – a kind of soft, wire wool, of which there are several brands on the market. This cleans them easily and makes them very bright. They should be absolutely clean inside *and* out; a blackened cooking vessel means waste of heat and time. You might keep a little of the scouring material always at hand near the sink in a small jam or cream pot.)

To continue:

1 wire basket for deep frying, to fit one of the large saucepans.

*1 colander.

*1 mincer – Always keep very clean in every part.

*1 grater. You might buy the spoon variety, a spoon with holes on one side for draining and with the other side rough for grating.

1 sink tidy.

1 kettle – two, if possible, one large, one small.

1 pair of scales. This is very desirable, but a really good pair of household scales is an expensive thing to buy, and you can manage without it by adopting the measurements given in the Introductory Notes, page 17.

1 pint measure. This is also very useful, and much less expensive than scales. But you can manage without it by adopting the liquid measurements given on page 17.

1 whisk, for beating eggs, cream, etc. This is by no means absolutely necessary, as many people can whisk very fast and thoroughly with a fork, and prefer to do so.

1 parsley chopper. This, again, is invaluable to some, to others, who always use a knife, more trouble than it is worth. If you use a knife to chop parsley, or anything else, hold the point of the knife against the board with one hand while with the other you move the heavier handle end lightly and quickly up and down.

1 apple corer. This is not essential, but useful and very cheap.

*1 tin opener.

*1 fish-slice or strainer spoon with holes in it, to lift out things which must be drained.

*1 set of steel knitting-needles, or skewers. Keep these very clean and use them for gently testing vegetables or cakes. It is far better to do this than to prod your food with a fork when testing it.

*1 vegetable forcer, a small bag with a nozzle attached through which you can squeeze potato *purée*, etc., when you want to arrange it neatly on a dish. This is very cheap. Keep it very clean.

1 vegetable ricer. This is a rather clumsy and expensive utensil and is now slightly out of fashion and favour. It is, however, useful for serving up potatoes or vegetables in a light, dry, airy state. See that anything that goes into it is well-drained and dried.

*1 set of graduated kitchen spoons (not wood).

*1 set of wooden spoons. Dedicate one, if you can, to sauces and one to fruit.

*2 kitchen forks, more if you like.

*3 kitchen knives, of different sizes. Keep these always very sharp.

*1 knife sharpener. This can be bought in a small, cheap, handy shape, and will last for ever.

*1 pastry-knife.

*1 pastry-brush.

*1 pastry-board.

*1 rolling-pin.

*1 large bowl to make pastry in.

*1 chopping board. Do NOT USE YOUR PASTRY BOARD FOR THIS.

*2 sieves, one hair, one wire. The hair sieve is needed for very fine sifting. Use the wire one for sifting flour or rubbing through fine crumbs.

*1 gravy strainer. This is invaluable for quick strain-
   ing, when the larger sieve would be a nuisance.
1 pestle and mortar. This is not essential, but it is
   a boon to the cook who has it.
*1 pair of scissors. These are absolutely essential
   to any cook who wants to work quickly and
   with a minimum of fuss, dirt and waste. Keep
   them always very clean. They should be of
   stainless metal and need not be very sharp.
   Use them for picking vegetables, such as
   spinach, spring greens, etc.; cutting the rind off
   bacon; cutting the skin between sausages and
   many other things for which a knife is clumsy.
*1 set of 3, or more, enamel or china basins.
*2 enamel mugs (one breakfastcup size, one teacup).
*1 set of enamel plates.
*1 tin charlotte mould, medium size.
*1 plain china mould – or decorated, if you like,
   but turrets, domes and birds' nests are better
   absent, though plenty of shops will still try to
   persuade you to buy them.
*1 china *soufflé* dish.
*1 set of earthenware ramekins or small china
   soufflé dishes.
  *As many fireproof cooking vessels as you can pos-
   sibly lay your hands on or find space to keep in
   the kitchen. These are now cheap and en-
   chantingly attractive. You can buy them in all
   sizes and colours as well as in fireproof glass.
   Food cooked in these dishes is nourishing,

23

tastes delicious and is very little trouble to prepare. How many you buy must depend on how much you want to spend and what room you have to spare, but do have at least three – one flat, one deeper, and one really deep round or oval-shaped one. The two latter, and if possible all three, should have lids. Serve all food cooked in fireproof dishes in the dishes themselves. (Another advantage – the ardours of dishing up are done away with.)

* Muslin for squeezing fruit juice, and tying up herbs.

It is worth while keeping a set of grapefruit or custard glasses always in the kitchen, as you may constantly need them for cold sweets.

Trays are rather a problem. Many of the prettiest are hopelessly unsuitable for their work; they show stains at once and need endless cleaning. It is worth while getting a plain oval tray painted with one of the new very hard glazes which persistently resist dirt and heat and only need wiping over to keep perfectly clean. They are also quite cheap and very light to handle.

Cleaning and washing utensils and materials you will probably decide on according to your own experience. But a few things are worth remembering.

(1) Always keep the sink clean. Use scouring powder in moderation to take away stains. Wipe off as much fat as possible from dirty dishes, knives,

24

forks, spoons and cooking vessels before washing them; if you habitually loose all this fat into the sink it will tend to block up the pipe and will certainly make everything smelly and difficult to clean.

(2) Wash up as much as possible in very hot water. Use some kind of soap or soap flakes in the water. Dry as much as you can with warm cloths. Keep your dish cloths very clean. Never use drying cloths for glass when they are getting old – they will leave smears and threads on the glass. COLD WATER gives glass a brilliant shine – if the cloths used to dry it are really dry themselves.

(3) If you want your silver to look dazzling, without constantly having to clean it, wash it always in warm water, then stand it, until it can be dried, in a pot or bowl of water as near boiling point as you can get it. Take the silver straight out of this water to dry.

B – STORES

In the first place, the absolutely essential flavourings which you must never run out of in the kitchen are three:

SALT.

PEPPER.

SUGAR.

Keep these three things always in stock, for whatever else you may or may not need, you will always need them. Cooking salt, which you can buy very cheaply in blocks, should be broken up and kept in a large enamel box with a lid. This box might well live near the cooker. It is useful to have smaller amounts of salt in a sprinkler for seasoning.

White pepper, the usual kind for cooking, can also be kept in bulk in a tin while a smaller amount is kept in a sprinkler. Paprika (coralline pepper) and cayenne can be bought in smaller quantities in sprinklers, ready for use in the kitchen. A sprinkler is also useful for sugar, but by no means necessary. It is convenient to have four kinds of sugar always in store, besides any special coffee sugar you may like to use. The four kinds are:

LOAF SUGAR.

WHITE SUGAR, either castor (fine) or granulated (coarse), or both.

BROWN SUGAR, either demerara (golden and crisp) or moist (paler, more like fine sand). Demerara is the more useful.

ICING SUGAR.

All sugar should be kept in tins or glazed china pots with lids.

Further stores that should always be kept in stock if you are going to cook regularly are:

FLOUR. Keep this covered in a dry place. If you are a small household, buy about three pounds at a time.

BAKING POWDER (unless you use a self-raising flour). Keep this in the tin in which you buy it. (A quarter-pound tin is plenty.)

RICE. When you buy this, say whether you want it specially for puddings or for curries and plain

26

boiling. Carolina rice is best for puddings and sweet dishes – Patna for curries and plain boiling.

MUSTARD. Remember that there is such a thing as French mustard, ready-made in pots, extremely good and easy to keep for some time.

VINEGAR. There are various kinds of vinegar. Malt vinegar is very cheap. Wine vinegar is more expensive and better. Tarragon vinegar is more expensive still and has a special, pleasant flavour. Unless you particularly like tarragon vinegar, you would do best to keep a pint bottle of wine vinegar in stock. A dash of vinegar keeps white vegetables white and helps to make meat and poultry tender.

OIL. Buy a good quality olive oil for preference. A pint bottle is a good size. Vegetable oil for frying may be bought in cans and fries extremely well if you like the flavour, which some people think delicious and others cannot abide.

HERBS (dried). You can either buy these all mixed together or in separate packets or bottles. Ideally, of course, one would always have fresh herbs at hand when cooking, for there is hardly any dish containing fish, meat or poultry that is not improved by being flavoured with a bouquet of fresh herbs. If you have a garden, or even a window-box, grow some herbs. Parsley, mint and thyme are all free and hardy growers. Sage, if left to itself, will riot everywhere. A small bush of bay is a blessing beyond compare. But if you live in a town and can do none of these things, then at least keep yourself well supplied with parsley, have a bottle of mixed dried herbs (which will last for a very long time) and a packet of dried bay leaves as well.

When you want to flavour anything with the herbs, tie them up in a piece of muslin and put this boldly into the saucepan or casserole, taking care to withdraw it before you serve the dish.

GELATINE. Ideally, again, one would probably not use anything here but freshly-boiled calves' feet. However, life is short and good quality gelatine is sold in leaves at a very reasonable price. A packet of very good quality leaves – each about three by nine inches – lasts a long time, costs about three shillings, and works out at not more than a penny for four sheets. Or it can be bought in smaller quantities. Keep it in a tin or wrapped carefully in greaseproof paper.

CORNFLOUR. Once the standby of the inferior cook and so held up to endless mockery to-day. Cornflour is good stuff, however, when used in the right place and the right way, and it is worth keeping a small packet in stock.

RENNET is used for making junket. Keep a small bottle in stock, if you like junket.

BREADCRUMBS. You can buy browned breadcrumbs in small and economical packets from the grocer. They save a lot of trouble and make a good, even coating when you are cooking such things as

Escalopes of Veal. You can also make bread-crumbs by drying scraps of bread or toast very slowly in the oven, then crushing them with the rolling-pin and storing them in covered tins.

RAISINS. If you like curry, pilaff or baked apples stuffed with raisins, keep a small packet of these in stock.

GOLDEN SYRUP. Besides being useful for treacle tart and puddings, this makes an economical binding for puddings and cakes if it is dissolved in milk and rather less sugar than usual is used. It is said that one tablespoonful dissolved in half a pint of milk is equal to three eggs.

WORCESTER SAUCE. Some people adore this as a flavouring, and it is useful, too, as a browning agent in gravy.

ANCHOVY ESSENCE. Again, some people like this flavour with fish.

TOMATO KETCHUP. This is useful for flavouring, or if you are fond of savouries.

CURRY POWDER. Keep a small tin in stock.

ALMONDS. These can be bought inexpensively in small quantities and kept for a long time. They are quickly skinned by being dropped into boiling water and left for a minute or so.

LEMON PEEL OR ORANGE PEEL. You can pare this off finely with a sharp knife, taking care not to cut off the white underskin, dry it in a slow oven and then store it in covered tins. It will keep for a long time and flavour things very pleasantly. It is particularly good with stewed apples, black-berries and damsons.

MUSHROOM STALKS. If you are cooking mushrooms and do not want to use the stalks, then peel them with care, dry them in a slow oven and use them when you want to flavour soups or stocks.

SPICES that are useful include:

NUTMEG. Buy a few nutmegs (they cost about 1½d. for two); keep them in a tin and grate them as you need them. Some cooks spoil everything with nut-meg – but discreetly used it is delicious.

MACE. Keep a very small tin in stock.

CINNAMON. Keep a very small tin in stock.

GROUND GINGER. Keep a very small tin in stock.

CLOVES. You can buy these either whole or ground. It is best to have them whole, as then they can be removed; besides, you can't stick an onion with ground cloves.

VANILLA. A stick of Vanilla is about nine inches long and costs about ninepence. You can break off half an inch at a time, use it, wash it, dry it and use it again several times. You may prefer to use vanilla essence, which can be bought in bottles, and should be used SPARINGLY, as it is stronger than you might think.

DECORATIVE INGREDIENTS worth keeping in stock are:

CHOPPED OR GROUND PISTACHIO NUTS. You can buy these in very small quantities.

CHOCOLATE HAILSTONES, OR SEMOLINA. These tiny

chocolate decorations taste good, look attractive, and can be bought by weight. Half a pound, stored in an air-tight tin, would last almost for ever.

Such further stores as TEA, COFFEE, JAM, MARMALADE, HONEY, etc., must be left to individual choice. Only remember that, unless you have a grinder of your own, you should buy your coffee freshly ground and in small quantities (about a quarter of a pound at a time) so that it does not have time to lose flavour before you have finished it.

Try leaving a sprig of dried rosemary in your tea-caddy; it will give an aromatic flavour to the tea.

If you get tired of a pot of jam, see if it will not prove more winning as part of a sweet.

There are certain perishable stores such as milk, butter and lard which should be cleared out regularly, and, in a small household, only bought in such small quantities as are strictly needed. A little calculation will always tell you how much this is likely to be. BUTTER is now so cheap that you can afford to use it constantly in cooking, but remember that although it is excellent for any preliminary frying of meat or vegetables and invaluable in sauces, soups, cakes and certain kinds of pastry, BUTTER IS NOT THE IDEAL FRYING MEDIUM. If you are frying something as a sole preparation for eating it you must generally use some other fat, for butter melts at a very low temperature and consequently does not fry so fast and thoroughly as, for instance, lard, which is an almost ideal frying fat – silent, clean and efficient. Margarine is too watery and spits over everything; dripping is apt to spit a lot and mutton dripping has a distinct, unpleasing taste; oil is excellent for frying. Altogether you would be well advised to stock chiefly butter, lard and oil. Butter has a dozen uses. Lard you will use for short crust pastry and frying, oil for frying.

Whenever, as a result of roasting or frying, you have some fat to pour off, pour a little boiling water into it as soon as you can. This will clarify and preserve it. Do not mix different kinds of fat together and do not keep your kitchen full of cups and basins with a little bit of old dripping in the bottom of each. Keep what you want and throw away what you don't or give it to someone who does. Fat is easiest to dispose of if you let it get cold in a basin. then it can be scooped out in a solid mass.

Look over your stores at regular intervals. No matter how small your store-cupboard may be, you will learn something by being thoroughly acquainted with it. Keep it clean and see that it has always got a little of everything you want in it. Nothing is more bleak than to visit a house where one can almost smell the bare cupboard boards – nothing more revolting than the kitchen that is all bits and ends of this and that: old fish dripping, dead parsley, a little mouldering jam at the bottom of a dish, a vast bin of damp flour, a few withered oranges, and on the shelves a regiment of veteran tins full of stores that are never used and never will be.

CHAPTER II

TIME is an ever-brooding nightmare to the beginner in cooking. Try how one will, it seems impossible at first to have everything cooked and ready for the table at the same moment. The meat runs ahead of the vegetables, the sweet – intended to be cool and refreshing – is still steaming warmly five minutes before dinner. Suddenly one remembers that plates and dishes have not been warmed and they are thrust into a glowing oven – and cracked. Gravy, too, presents a last-moment problem that leaves the novice with sticky hands, fat-spotted clothes and burning face, clashing her distracted way among the dishes while the meat delights to coat itself in cold grease and the vegetables to boil over on to the stove.

Do not despair at this dark picture. In an amazingly short time it will become almost an instinct to start cooking food at the right moment, so that the various ingredients of a meal are marshalled exactly to time. Try following the time-tables in this book and see whether you are a slow, average or quick worker. Take individual recipes and work out times for yourself, remembering that these will vary

33

according to the type of cooker you use, and that the time of year and temperature of your kitchen will affect the time which it takes for a cold sweet to set and even to some extent your own capacity for working quickly.

The first thing you must do is to assemble all the utensils and ingredients necessary for a particular dish. Weigh out all your ingredients and put them aside. Get out saucepans, fireproof dishes, etc. Take out your chopping-board, if you will need it, and see that it is clean. Have salt, pepper and sugar handy. Put the colander in the sink and a plate or some paper on which you can rest dirty knives, forks or spoons close by the stove. Sieve any flour you may want. See that some greaseproof paper is at hand if you want to cover a saucepan very closely. Cover any surface on which you are going to trim or peel vegetables, beat eggs, and so on, with several layers of newspaper. Then, as you accumulate refuse, you can pick up one or two thicknesses of paper complete with the mess upon it, and put it in the fire or dustbin, leaving fresh newspaper underneath. Remember that you may want one or two clean dry cloths to fold over dishes towards the end of your cooking.

All this may sound a counsel of unnecessary perfection to the experienced cook – it is salvation for the beginner who MUST concentrate upon the work in hand, once she has begun, without frantic searches for this, that or the other missing utensil or ingredient.

As soon as you begin to grow more confident about the actual cooking of a meal, you may find that you can work with one eye on the food while you are engaged in whipping eggs or cream, chopping parsley, preparing vegetables or washing up saucepans and dishes. But don't anticipate this stage in the beginning, or you will have some bad moments.

Suppose, next, that you know how to prepare a meal in time. You have studied the recipe, followed the time-table and all is ready except your guests, who have not arrived. The food begins to go into a decline beneath your eyes. This is a maddening experience, even for someone whose only responsibility is the cooking of the meal; it is sheer torture at first for the cook-hostess-parlourmaid. Unless, however, you have indulged in such things as *soufflés* or omelettes, there is no reason for despair. Most of the meals in this book can be postponed for a certain length of time without being damaged. Here are a few tips on how to keep back food without ruining it.

Keep potatoes, rice, or any vegetables that have been steamed or boiled in a saucepan close to a low flame with a little butter softly melting into them, and a dry cloth folded above the saucepan to absorb any moisture.

Put fried or grilled food in a closed fireproof dish in the bottom of the oven at a very low heat.

Stand gravy in a dish in a pan of gently boiling

water; or put the bowl over a saucepan of steaming water.

Replenish the water in the saucepan over which anything is steaming with BOILING water, if it is running short.

If anything is becoming over-cooked in the oven, take it out, leaving the oven flame on, turn the grill on UPWARDS and place the food on a covered dish between these two sources of heat, i.e., under the grill. If this is impossible, put it in a covered dish on the plate-rack above the stove with not too fierce a flame beneath. NEVER GARNISH ANYTHING WITH GREEN STUFF SUCH AS WATERCRESS, PARSLEY OR MINT UNTIL THE LAST MOMENT. If garnishings don't look completely fresh and crisp, they are much better absent.

A good all-embracing counsel for housewives in these distressing circumstances is: 'Turn all heat low, keep everything covered and have two or three clean, dry cloths at hand.'

One of the most important things to remember in getting a meal ready is to leave time somewhere for laying the table. This takes anything from five to ten minutes. It is really most satisfactory to lay the table before starting to cook, but if you come in late and in a hurry and have to start on a dish right away, it will be impossible to do this. In nearly every case, therefore, a space has been found in the time-table for laying the table while cooking the meal. It is a wise rule never to leave the kitchen while anything is boiling fast. Take, for example, rice. Unless you are at hand to keep your eye on it and give it an occasional stir, rice delights in two forms of mischief. Either it will rise in a sudden surge of foam and boil over or, if you have turned down the heat in the hope of keeping it boiling steadily, it will just go off the boil altogether and coagulate in little heaps at the bottom of the pan, so throwing out all your calculation as to the time for cooking it. The same applies to simmering thick sauces. Don't leave them for a moment. Somewhere, however, during the preparation of every meal, there comes an interval of peace when food is quietly simmering in saucepan or casserole and you can safely leave it for a short time to its own devices. These intervals are always marked on the time-tables in big type – don't, unless you are very sure of yourself, waste them in mending a ladder in your stockings, plucking your eyebrows or doing a little telephoning. *Lay the table* and, if you still have some free time, *wash up*.

Washing up as you go along saves an endless amount of trouble. In the first place, it clears the kitchen; it it wonderfully calming to the mind to dispose of mess as you go along. Knives, forks, saucepans, etc., once they are washed, can be used again if necessary at a later stage in preparing the meal, instead of cluttering up the sink and draining-board. If they are not likely to be wanted again, put them back in their proper places – and *everything* in the kitchen should have its own allotted place. If you let chaos mount around you in a small kitchen you may find when the time comes to dish up dinner that there is no space left to do it in. This will probably lead to frantic gymnastics, such as moving bowls of hot fat with your elbow or butting aside saucepans with your head. A friend of the authors' once had a tiny, cramped kitchen that always became over-crowded while she was cooking; space was so important, and her hands in consequence always so full, that she acquired the dangerous habit (NOT recommended to readers in similar circumstances), of turning the electric light switch on and off with her tongue.

Another reason for washing up as you go along is that cooking utensils, saucepans, dishes, etc., which are easy enough to clean if you start on them straight away generally become much harder to wash if you leave them for a few hours. Remnants of sauce will cling to the sides and bottom of saucepans, morsels of potato and milk become adhesive as sticking-plaster, anything which has been in contact with fish rapidly turns into a gluey abomination, and eggs, vegetables and fruits leave stains on knives and forks that turn black and take twice as long to remove.

Always wash knives, forks and spoons that have been in contact with fish or onions in cold water. Anything greasy should be wiped over with newspaper and the paper burnt or put into the dustbin. Wash anything that has held milk in cold water. Fill dirty saucepans with hot water and leave them to soak.

Wash up, therefore, as much as you can, and put anything which you have no time to wash 'in soak', and return all washed objects to their proper place.

All this may sound rather trivial advice, but if it is not followed a small kitchen will soon become unbearably cluttered up, while the owner complains to her friends that cooking is such a wearisome, messy business that no *intelligent* woman can be bothered to waste her time over it.

Another thing to remember is that dishes and plates won't warm themselves. In order to make these hot, put them in the rack above the stove, if anything is boiling below, and cover them with a clean dry cloth. If you are doing all your cooking in the oven, lower the flame there for a few minutes before dishing up and put the plates and dishes at the bottom of the oven. If you are cooking both above and below, you can leave the plates under the grill; they will warm quickly here, but you must take care not to let anything boil over on to them.

Remember that food cooked in casseroles has generally become so hot that the plates on which it is to go need not be so warm as those that are to contain grilled or fried dishes; the latter should always be particularly hot.

The anxieties of dishing up depends very much on the particular meal one is cooking. Sometimes one can leave the kitchen with a light heart when guests arrive, confident that the food is quietly cooking behind one's back. Sometimes the last moments of preparation for dinner are all a wild flurry. It will help if you put anything that is to be eaten cold ready on a tray beforehand, but it may be that everything is to be eaten hot. Perhaps a sauce has to be prepared at the last moment, vegetables collected in dishes and preparations made for keeping a hot sweet until it is wanted. In this case, *don't fear* A BOLD INTERVAL. Don't hurry a sauce and spoil it, or fling food roughly into dishes so that it looks unappetising. Keep cool, move quietly and deliberately. Nobody will mind a few minutes' delay at the beginning of dinner that may make all the difference to the food itself. But if you start to rush, you will almost certainly make a noise; the clash of pans like cymbals in the kitchen will not only rack your guests' nerves but horrify them, if they are kindly souls, by its suggestion that the meal entails a terrible effort on your part.

Finally, all but super-women should wash and tidy themselves just before bringing dinner in. Even the calmest may look flushed and wild after a bout of cooking in a small kitchen. All-over aprons keep one clean from cooking stains, but are rather hot to wear, and a small apron that just covers the front of the clothes is all that is necessary unless you are a natural spiller. Never cook with dangling sleeves or floppy wrist-bows. Some women can wear rubber gloves and move about untainted among fish, onions and greasy water. These gloves are quite cheap and anyone who has never worn them should buy a pair and see how she likes them. If she decides, like many others, that one might as well try to cook in a pair of boxing-gloves, she will at least have had a few days of uncomfortable purity before returning to the old ways. People who care for their hands keep a bottle of lotion near the sink. Lemon is good for removing stains, and so is any form of peroxide solution, which will also take away smells of fish, onions, etc.

One word more. Whenever you are cooking you will probably find that you have such things as bones, trimmings, rabbit heads, giblets, etc., left over. Don't throw these away, but make time, if you possibly can, to put them into a saucepan with plenty of cold water, pepper and salt. Add any scraps of vegetables, odd tomatoes, left over potatoes or rice, etc., celery heads, or herbs of any description. Bring very gently to the boil, and allow it all to simmer quietly in the background while you do the rest of your cooking. The longer and more slowly it simmers, the better it will be, and the result will be STOCK.

Stock is invaluable to the cook. You can use it as a basis for soup, adding any flavouring or vegetables you like. You can use it for gravy. Whenever a recipe says 'add water or stock', you should use stock if you possibly can. Strain it when it is cooked, and boil it up again gently whenever you want it. But do not keep it a moment after any faintly sour smell comes from it. Stock made from vegetables does not keep as long as that made from meat alone.

CHAPTER III

Spring Menu No. 1   For Four People

LAMB CUTLETS MAINTENON
(COOKED WITH ONION AND CHEESE)
NEW POTATOES
YOUNG CARROTS

MOUSSE OF CHOCOLATE

This menu takes advantage of the young spring vegetables which should be at their best. Eggs, which should be cheap at this time of year, are used in the sweet. English cutlets would be too expensive to include in the menu, and therefore New Zealand lamb, whose merits are now admitted even by the most supercilious cooks, is used instead.

SEVEN DINNERS FOR SPRING

Lamb Cutlets Maintenon. (Cost: about 2/5½.)

7 or 8 lamb cutlets	3 ozs. butter
2 onions	1 oz. flour
¼ lb. cooking cheese	½ pint milk
Pepper, salt	

Buy a piece of best end of New Zealand neck of lamb, with seven or eight small cutlets in it. Get the butcher to trim the cutlets.

Peel and quarter two medium-sized onions and put them in a small saucepan with salted water to cover. Close the lid and cook for 45 minutes, not too fast or the water will boil over.

While the onion is cooking, grate a quarter of a pound of cooking cheese on to a plate. Heat half a pint of milk in a saucepan and keep it warm but not boiling. Fifteen minutes before the onion will have finished cooking, start to make a white sauce. Melt one ounce of butter in a saucepan: when it is all melted and hissing add a tablespoonful of flour and stir it into the butter. Take the saucepan to the edge of the stove and add, little by little, the half pint of milk which you have warmed, stirring vigorously all the time. When all the milk is added and the sauce is perfectly smooth, replace the saucepan on the flame and cook gently, still stirring, until it boils. Add the grated cheese and let the sauce continue to boil, while you stir, for five or six minutes. Then remove the saucepan again to the edge of the stove.

Now turn your attention to the onions, which

43

should·be cooked. Put a gravy strainer in a large bowl. Pour out the onions into the strainer; the liquid will run through, the onions remain. Squash them thoroughly against the side of the strainer with a wooden spoon (you can use the one with which you stirred the white sauce) until they almost form a paste. Now mix them with any liquid in the bowl and add to the sauce. Stir thoroughly and season, tasting. Leave by the edge of the stove.

Put two ounces of butter to heat in a saucepan. While the butter is melting, rub the cutlets on either side with a little pepper and salt. When the butter sizzles all over, put in the cutlets, almost cover the saucepan with the lid and let the cutlets cook for six minutes. You must turn them once during this time. After six minutes, take them out and arrange them in an overlapping circle at the bottom of a fireproof dish. Give the sauce a final brisk stirring and pour it over the cutlets. They should completely disappear beneath the creamy mixture. Cook in the oven at a moderate heat for about 30 minutes, leaving the lid of the dish off so that the top may just brown here and there.

RECIPE 2.

New Potatoes. (Cost: about 6d.)

1½ lbs. new potatoes	A little butter
A little mint	Salt
A little parsley	

Wash and scrape a pound and a half of new potatoes, and put them into boiling salted water with

44

a little piece of mint. Boil fairly fast for fifteen to twenty minutes, with the lid off, and then test them gently with a knitting-needle. (The prongs of a fork might damage a young potato.) As soon as they are done, turn them into a colander to drain, and remove the mint. Put them into a hot dish with a little melted butter and sprinkle over them a very little chopped parsley. Keep the lid of the dish on.

A good way of buttering the potatoes is to cover them with the paper which was wrapped round half a pound of butter, or with an inverted butter dish from which nearly all the butter has been used. This is a most satisfactory and economical way of using up dreary little ends of butter, for turning the dish upside down on the potatoes is much easier and cleaner than scraping the dish – the steam from the potatoes melts every scrap of butter from the dish.

RECIPE 3.

Young Carrots. (Cost: about 8d.)

| 1 bundle young carrots | Butter |
| Salt, pepper | A little parsley |

Buy a bundle of young carrots. They should be a bright colour and quite stiff, not dull and flabby. Wash them, scrape them gently and dry them. Reheat the butter in which the cutlets were cooked, and when it is hot put in the carrots. Cook gently with the lid closed for about twenty minutes. Test with a knitting-needle. When cooked place in a warm dish. Pour over any butter that is left, season and sprinkle with a little finely chopped parsley.

RECIPE 4.

Mousse of Chocolate. (Cost: about 1/4.)

¼ lb. bitter chocolate   4d. cream
4 eggs

Buy a quarter of a pound of bitter chocolate or, if your favourite kind is only sold by the half pound, buy a half pound, break it in two and put away one half in a tin.

Heat the oven. When it is warm, place the chocolate in a basin or saucepan in the oven and let it get soft. Keep the oven heat low. As soon as the chocolate is soft but NOT melting – that is to say, when it is flabby, as it would be if you left it lying in the sun on a warm day – take it out. Meanwhile, you have separated the yolks of four eggs from the whites by cracking each egg against the edge of a bowl and allowing the white to drip down into the bowl while you pour the yolk from one half of the shell to the other. Whip the whites stiffly with a fork – not as stiffly as for a *meringue* but for about five minutes. Beat the yolks very slightly and while the slab of chocolate is still soft and hot, add the yolks and beat well together. Then add the stiffly whipped whites. Stir thoroughly.

Pour into a glass dish to set, or, if you prefer, into separate glasses or china ramekins. Decorate by pouring over the chocolate fourpennyworth of un-whipped, unsweetened cream, and adding any decoration, such as crystallised rose-leaves or chocolate semolina that you may happen to have.

This dish, which is quite easy to make, is deliciously light and sweet, BUT – if you let the chocolate start melting at the beginning it will be sticky and rather greasy. It sets very quickly even on the hottest day – in about thirty minutes – but it will be all the lighter if it stands for a few hours before being eaten.

SHOPPING LIST

						s.	d.
Butcher.							
Best end of New Zealand neck, containing 7 or 8 cutlets ...	...	...	...	...	...	1	10
Dairy.							
½ pint milk	...	...	...	...	...	0	1½
4 eggs	...	...	...	...	...	0	6
Cream	...	...	...	...	...	0	4
Greengrocer.							
1½ lbs. new potatoes		...	...	...		0	6
1 bundle young carrots		...	...	...		0	8
Grocer.							
¼ lb. cooking cheese	...	...	...	...		0	2
¼ lb. bitter chocolate	...	...	...	...		0	6
From Stock.							
2 onions ...	...	...	...	...	...	0	1
3 ozs. butter	...	...	...	...	...	0	3
Flour, parsley and decoration for sweet				...		0	0½
						5	0

DINNERS FOR BEGINNERS

TIME-TABLE

Dinner at Eight O'Clock

N.B. – If you are dining at a different time, calculate from the time-table at what hour you will have to start your preparations and then alter the hands of the kitchen clock to conform with the time-table. You will find it easier than making individual calculations over every item.

———

The sweet should be made before you start on the rest of the dinner; if you have any doubts about it, it would be wise to make it in the morning. If you make it in the evening you should start at a quarter to six, or two and a quarter hours before dinner-time.

5 45   Make sweet and wash up.
6 15   Wash and scrape potatoes.
       Wash and scrape carrots.
       Peel onions.
6 30   *Start cooking onions for sauce.*
       Grate cheese on to plate.

Lay Table. Don't Forget You have Just been handling Onions

7 0   *Start making white sauce.*
7 15   Set sauce at edge of stove.
       Strain and mash onions, mix with liquid, add to sauce, season and keep at edge of stove.
7 20   *Light oven.*
       Heat butter to cook cutlets.
       Rub cutlets with salt and pepper.
7 23   *Start cooking cutlets.*
7 26   *Turn cutlets.*

SEVEN DINNERS FOR SPRING

7 28   *Start boiling salted water for potatoes.*

7 29   *Take out cutlets,* arrange in fireproof dish, stir sauce and pour over cutlets. Place in oven to finish cooking. Put saucepan in which sauce was cooking to soak.

7 33   *Reheat butter* in which cutlets were cooked for carrots. Dry carrots.

7 35   *Start cooking carrots.*

7 40   *Start boiling potatoes.*

       Wash, dry and chop parsley. Divide in two portions.

       Pour cream over sweet and decorate.

7 55   *Test potatoes.* If cooked, drain and when dry put in warm dish. Add butter. Sprinkle over chopped parsley. Cover with lid.

7 59   Turn out carrots into warm dish, season and pour over liquid from saucepan. Sprinkle with chopped parsley. Cover with lid.

PUT PLATES AND DISHES TO WARM

If people are late, you can leave the cutlets in the oven. Cover the dish in which they are cooking and turn down the oven as low as possible. The potatoes will be all right in the vegetable dish if you keep it hot, but the carrots had better not be turned out of the saucepan, which should be set at the edge of the stove to keep thoroughly hot.

49

ESCALOPES OF VEAL WITH VEGETABLES
(PEAS, TOMATOES)
BROWNED POTATO PUREE

LEMON PIE

Here is a meal that is very easy to serve, for the whole of the first course is arranged on one big dish – and very sightly it looks. This is a great advantage to the single-handed hostess, as guests can help themselves and conversation run on unimpeded by a perpetual circling of dishes.

RECIPE I.
Escalopes of Veal with Vegetables. (Cost: about 3/9½.)

8 slices (about 1 lb.) fillet of veal	3 ozs. butter
2 lbs. potatoes (old)	1 lemon
1 tin peas (or 1 lb. new peas)	1 egg
½ lb. tomatoes	Browned crumbs
Pepper, salt	Little milk

Escalopes of veal are very thin slices of fillet of veal. Ask your butcher to cut you eight thin slices of fillet of veal. Unless he is used to doing this, as some, but by no means all, butchers are (in Soho, for example), he will probably try and cut the slices too thick. So, as he poises his knife, you must look keenly and say in your most persuasive tones, 'Thinner than that, please,' until your slices are only about a quarter of an inch thick – just as thin, in fact, as they can be cut. As a rule, the butcher will flatten them for you, but in any case, you had better flatten them again at home by banging them with a rolling-pin. Whatever you do, never order escalopes of veal by telephone or proxy, unless you are certain that your butcher understands exactly what you want – you must see them being cut yourself.

Squeeze out and strain the juice of a lemon. Beat up an egg for a minute with a fork and put it on an enamel plate. On a second plate put plenty of bread-crumbs, seasoned with a little pepper and salt. (The best kind of crumbs for this purpose are those which you can buy at the grocer's, ready-made and in cheap packets, but, if you have none or prefer a stricter economy, you can make your own by drying odd slices of bread very slowly in the oven, then crushing them with a rolling-pin and storing them in a tin. Never coat anything which you are about to fry in fresh breadcrumbs.)

Trim the slices of veal into neat shapes, about the size of the palm of your hand, and flatten them with a rolling-pin. Dip each slice first in the egg and then in the seasoned breadcrumbs. Heat two ounces of butter (or lard, or bacon fat) in a frying-pan and when it is melted and sizzling (or, in the case of lard, smoking very lightly) put in the slices of veal. After about five or six minutes, during which you have brooded over them, shifting them slightly or shaking the pan to ensure even cooking, turn the slices and cook them for the same length of time on the other side. The slices are so thin that they will not take long to cook. Test them, by cutting off one corner with a very sharp knife and eating the veal. When the meat is almost cooked, sprinkle a little of the strained lemon juice over it. Lift out the slices with a fish-slice and rest them on some soft paper on an enamel plate; the paper will drain off any superfluous fat. Cover the plate with another plate or a saucepan lid and put it in the bottom of the oven at low heat to await the final dishing-up. If you are unable to fry all the slices of veal at once, the first batch can be kept waiting in this way while you cook the second.

VEGETABLES. (TOMATOES, PEAS, POTATOES.)

Tomatoes.

Wipe eight small tomatoes and cut them into halves. Make the butter in which you cooked the veal very hot, adding a little more butter if there is very little left. Fry the tomatoes lightly in the butter, taking the flat side without skin first. They will take about four minutes to cook. Lift them out with the fish-slice and put them with the veal.

Peas.

If you are having this meal in the early spring, fresh green peas will be rather expensive. (There is a recipe for cooking garden peas on pages 115 and 162.)

If you cannot afford fresh peas, you will find tinned ones perfectly satisfactory. Buy a small tin, and heat the peas according to the directions on the tin. It is usually best to heat them by piercing a hole in the top of the tin and then standing it in boiling water for ten minutes or a little longer. If you do this, the liquor with the peas will lose its jelly-like consistency and the peas themselves will be greener and firmer than if you take them straight out of the tin and then heat them. Grasp the tin with a cloth – it will be very hot – open it with a tin-opener, drain the peas and put them on the dish with the other vegetables in the way described below.

Potatoes.

Buy two pounds of old potatoes – the 'floury' kind – and peel them, cutting out very carefully any black marks or dubious places. Put them into a saucepan with enough cold water to cover them well and a tablespoonful of salt. Bring to the boil and boil with the lid almost closed until the potatoes are cooked – about twenty-five minutes from when you first put them in. Test with a fork or knitting-needle to see when they are done. Drain them well KEEPING THE WATER IN WHICH THEY WERE COOKED FOR MAKING GRAVY, dry the saucepan and return it to the edge of the flame with the potatoes in it so that they may dry very thoroughly. Now take a fork and mash them together with a slice of butter and a tablespoonful or two of milk. Keep on mashing until the potato *purée* is perfectly smooth and white, without a lump large or small. Season with pepper and salt, tasting. Now force the *purée* in lines on to a greased baking-sheet. (For less than a shilling you can buy a vegetable forcer and its little bag, through which you can force your potato in charming squiggles.) Now pop the baking-sheet into a quick oven and leave it for ten or fifteen minutes until the potatoes are browned on top.

N.B. – If you fail to mash your potatoes absolutely smooth, the smallest lumps will stick in the nozzle of the forcer and block it up, while the potato surges out at the wrong end of the bag.

Gravy.

In your frying-pan there will be a certain amount of tomato juice and fat. Stir this well round with a wooden spoon and add to it about a teacupful of the water in which the potatoes boiled. Taste, add pepper and salt, if necessary, and bring to the boil. When the gravy boils add a teaspoonful of lemon juice and simmer for a few minutes longer. Strain at the last moment and pour over the veal in the dish.

Assembling the dish.

Pile the veal in the middle of a large hot dish. Dispose the peas and tomatoes in little clumps around it. Lift your browned squiggles of potato off the baking-sheet with a fish-slice and arrange them round the veal and vegetables. Pour over the gravy. Pass the dish to your guests and allow each to help himself.

RECIPE 2.

Lemon Pie. (Cost: about 11d.)

8 ozs. flour	3 eggs
4 ozs. lard	6 ozs. castor sugar
¼ teaspoon baking powder	1 tablespoon cornflour
Pinch of salt	1 large lemon (or 2 little ones)

Make a short crust pastry case, as for a flan, using a flan tin, which you can buy very cheaply.

To make the pastry.

Sieve half a pound of flour into a basin together with a pinch of salt and a quarter of a teaspoonful of baking powder. If you have no sieve, use a gravy strainer, but this takes longer. Cut up four ounces of lard into pieces among the flour, rub these pieces lightly and quickly into the flour with the tips of your fingers, lifting the mixture so that the air may get into it, until the whole resembles fine breadcrumbs. Leave no unbroken lumps of fat, however small. Keep your ingredients cool, working them in the coolest part of the kitchen; if the mixture is allowed to get hot, the fat will melt and the pastry will be heavy, with a strong, fatty taste. As soon as all the fat is well rubbed in, make a little hole in the middle and pour into it about a dessertspoonful of cold water. Mix this in quickly with a pastry-knife. Add another two dessertspoonfuls of water and knead the mixture with the knuckles of your hands until it forms a firm ball of dough that leaves the sides of the basin quite clean. Turn out this ball on to a floured board and knead again for a minute, gently pressing cracks together as you turn the dough round and round. Flour your rolling-pin, standing it upright in the flour bin or jar, and roll out the pastry. Roll lightly and quickly in one direction and, in order to make a round of pastry, keep turning the pastry to your left and rolling away from you that portion which is directly in front of you.

The quantities given in this recipe will make a round of pastry about nine inches across and a quarter of an inch thick. This will fit a flan-tin measuring about eight inches across. Do not try to make the pastry fit a larger tin or, as you stretch it, it will split at the edges and the result will be a failure. Place the tin face downwards on the pastry and cut round the edge. You will be left with a ring of pastry about an inch wide; trim this round the edge and make it a little smaller and you can use it for the walls of the flan. First lift the round of pastry carefully and ease it gently into the bottom of the tin. Just moisten all round the edge with cold water – this will join the pastry making the floor to that making the rim; now put the inch-wide strip round the rim of the tin and wet it where it joins. If any pastry hangs over the edge of the tin, pare it off, cutting AWAY from you with the pastry-knife.

Line the flan with a piece of greaseproof paper rather larger than the flan itself. Weigh this paper down with a scattering of uncooked rice or beans, so that the floor of the flan may not rise as it cooks. Bake in a hot oven for twenty minutes, then take a look. When the pastry is a golden colour it is sufficiently cooked.

The Lemon Filling.

Separate the yolks from the whites of three eggs by cracking each egg against the side of a basin and allowing the white to drip down into the basin while you turn the yolk from one half of the shell to the other. Put the yolks in another basin and beat them for a minute or two. Add to them four tablespoonfuls of castor sugar, the rind and juice of a large juicy lemon (or two small ones) and a tablespoonful of sifted cornflour. Stir well together and pour into the top of a double boiler. Cook, stirring all the time, until the mixture thickens – this will take at least ten minutes. Take the boiler away from the heat and leave it by the edge of the stove while you beat up the three whites of egg to a stiff froth, china white in colour, which will cling so firmly to the basin that you might almost turn it upside down without the froth dropping out. This is hard work, whether you do it with a fork or a whisk, and will take you ten or fifteen minutes. Next, you must fold the lemon and egg mixture into the whites – pour in a little of the mixture at a time and mix the two with a pastry-knife, simply lifting them one over the other until at last the whites disappear and the lemon mixture becomes very pale. Pour this meringue mixture into the pastry case and return the tin to a hot oven for ten minutes. The lemon should brown very slightly on top. Don't be alarmed if the top falls slightly when you take it out of the oven.

This sweet is almost as good cold as hot, and warms up very well.

SHOPPING LIST

	s.	d.
Butcher.		
8 very thin slices (about 1 lb.) fillet of veal ...	2	4
Dairy.		
4 eggs	0	6
Greengrocer.		
2 lemons (large—or 3, if small)	0	3
½ lb. tomatoes	0	4
2 lbs. old potatoes	0	3
Grocer.		
1 small tin peas	0	5½
4 ozs. lard	0	2
From Stock.		
3 ozs. butter	0	3
½ lb. flour	0	1½
6 ozs. castor sugar	0	1
	4	9

Breadcrumbs, milk, cornflour, negligible, or at most ½d.

SEVEN DINNERS FOR SPRING

TIME-TABLE

Dinner at Eight O'Clock

N.B. – If you are dining at a different time, calculate from the time-table the hour at which you will have to start your preparations and then alter the hands of the kitchen clock to conform with the time-table. You will find it easier than making individual calculations over every item.

The lemon pie needs all your attention for about 45 minutes so that it would be as well to make it before you begin the rest of the cooking. It retains its heat for a long while and does not need to be piping hot. If you like to make it earlier, it is very good cold.

5 45   *Light oven for pastry*
      Make sweet and wash up.
6 40   *Turn out oven.* Put tart on rack.
      Peel potatoes.

Lay the Table
Put Plates and Dishes in Rack Ready for Heating

7 0   *Start boiling potatoes in cold salted water.*
      Wipe and halve tomatoes.
      Squeeze out lemon juice and strain.
      Prepare veal for frying.
      Grease baking-sheet.
7 25   *Light oven for potatoes.*
      Start boiling salted water for peas.
      Drain and dry potatoes. Keep water. Mash with milk, butter and seasoning, pass through forcer on to baking-sheet.

7 40   *Start cooking potato squiggles in oven.*
        Heat butter for veal.

7 42   *Start frying veal.*
        Start heating peas in hot water.

7 47   *Turn veal.*

7 52   *Lift out veal,* put in oven on soft paper, covered.
        Start frying tomatoes.

7 58   *Lift out tomatoes,* put with veal.
        Make gravy.

8 0   Open peas, drain. Assemble veal and vegetables
        on dish, pour strained gravy over.

If people are late, keep the veal and tomatoes covered in the bottom of the oven. Leave the potatoes on the sheet, but turn the oven heat very low. Let the peas remain in the tin, unopened, in hot water. On no account start assembling the dish until you are sure your guests have arrived.

SPRING CHICKEN

WATERCRESS

GRILLED TOMATOES

SAUTE POTATOES

RHUBARB PRINCESS

In spring and summer it is possible to find in the shops *petits poussins* selling for about 1/6d each. You might take advantage of this, and of the rosy sticks of young, forced rhubarb now appearing in the greengrocers' shops, to cook a simple and delicious meal.

RECIPE 1.

Spring Chicken with Watercress. (Cost: about 3/1½.)

2 poussins	Pepper, salt
1 tablespoonful olive oil	1 bundle watercress
1 dessertspoonful flour (for gravy)	

Buy two *petits poussins* – half for each person. The poulterer will draw and truss the birds and will give you the giblets if you remind him. These small chickens are delicious grilled, but it is rather difficult to manage this with the ordinary small grill, and you would be well advised to start by parboiling them, and then to give them a rapid browning under the grill.

Wash the giblets, cut away any superfluous fat or skin, and put them into plenty of salted water. Heat the water and, when it is very hot, but not yet boiling, add the chickens. Now bring the water to the boil again, and see that it does no more than simmer very gently for ten minutes.

Mix a tablespoonful of salt and half a teaspoonful of pepper on a plate. Pour a tablespoonful of olive oil into a cup.

When the chickens have simmered for ten minutes, take them out, drain them and let them cool for five minutes. Leave the giblets to continue simmering. Then remove the skewers and trussing strings and cut each chicken firmly in half along the breastbone with a large, sharp knife. Rub each half of chicken with some of the mixed seasoning and then paint it over on both sides with olive oil, using a pastry brush.

Light the oven and put a large fireproof dish in the bottom to warm. Make the grill very hot. When the grill is really hot, grill the chickens, two halves, or as much as you can conveniently manage, at a time. Turn each piece once – each side will take about three minutes. As soon as each half is cooked (it should look lightly browned and rather blistered) put it in the hot fireproof dish, close the lid and put the dish in the bottom of the oven, keeping the heat very low. You can leave the chicken in this dish until it is needed.

To serve, arrange the chicken in the middle of a

long, hot dish, with a liberal allowance of well-washed and carefully drained watercress and the grilled tomatoes at either end.

Gravy (if you like it. It is not usually served with a grill, but is good).

When you have finished grilling the tomatoes in the same pan as the chicken (see next recipe) you will find a certain amount of juice and fat in the bottom of the pan. If there is more than a table-spoonful of fat, pour it off until there is only that much left. Put the pan over a low flame and sprinkle in a pinch of pepper, half a teaspoonful of salt and a dessertspoonful of sieved flour. Stir all this well. Then, stirring all the time, add as much liquid from the saucepan in which the giblets are still simmering as you want gravy, and bring to the boil. Keep on scraping at the bottom and edges of the pan and squashing and stirring away lumps for all you are worth. The gravy will look pale, solid and unpromising at first, but as you work away at it it will gradually darken and become smooth. Allow it to boil gently for three or four minutes. Taste it and see if it is sufficiently seasoned.

To keep gravy hot either (1) stand it in a warm dish at the very bottom of the oven at very low heat or (2) stand the gravy dish over a saucepan of boiling water, or (3) fill up a baking dish with boiling water and stand the gravy dish in it over a low flame. GRAVY SHOULD ALWAYS BE VERY HOT.

N.B. – It is worth while studying this recipe carefully, as it shows the *method* of making gravy of all sorts, thick or thin. The basis of a gravy is always the fat and juices left in the bottom of a roasting, grilling or frying-pan when you have finished cooking the food which the gravy is to accompany. (Incidentally it is a considerable help in cleaning these dishes.) All but a small amount of fat should be poured away and you must take care that the dark sediment does not pour off with it, but remains in the pan. Leave about a tablespoonful of fat and juice. To this you must always add (1) seasoning, and (2) warm water or stock. If the gravy is to be thick – like the one above – you must add sieved flour and let it fry in the fat before adding the stock or water.

Gravy, as you can see, is a very simple thing to make. It needs two things: first, really vigorous stirring; second, a good simmer for some minutes after it boils. You will be surprised at the amount of dark juices that a spoon can scrape away from the bottom and sides of the most bare-looking pan after a roast or a fry; grilling provides a paler gravy and, if you like, you can darken or flavour it with some kind of gravy-browning or a few drops of Worcester sauce or tomato ketchup. But DON'T embark on the unnecessary and extravagant habit of making all your gravy with cubes or spoonfuls of meat extract. Water in which vegetables – particularly potatoes – have boiled, is excellent for use in gravy and should always be set aside if you are going to make gravy for the same meal. Remember that this water is salted.

The thing that makes gravy seem so difficult to accomplish, is that it is generally made at the last moment. But take it calmly and all will be well; at the most it can only hold you up for a few minutes. Remember to strain thin gravy before pouring it into a dish.

RECIPE 2.
Grilled Tomatoes. (Cost: about 5d.)
                1 lb. small tomatoes

Paint ten or twelve small tomatoes with the olive oil left over from the chickens, seat them in the bottom of the grilling pan and grill them on each side quickly until they blister and turn a light brown (but not black) on top. They will take about three minutes on each side. When cooked, lift them out gently on a strainer spoon and put them in the fireproof dish to keep warm with the chicken. Never mind if the tops split a little.

(It is after this that you make the gravy.)

RECIPE 3.
Sauté Potatoes. (Cost: about 2½d.)
    1 lb. potatoes   Salt   3 ozs. lard

These are made with cold, cooked potatoes. Buy a pound, peel them and put them whole into well-salted water. Bring to the boil and boil rather fast with the lid half on for about twenty minutes – test with a fork and see when they are soft, but NOT squashy. Drain them well and leave them on a plate until they are wanted. Then cut them into circular slices about as thick as a florin.

Heat a large piece of lard in a frying-pan – you will want at least two ounces and possibly three, and the lard, when melted, ought to be about half an inch deep in the pan. When a faint smoke rises from the pan, the fat is hot enough. Fry the potatoes fairly quickly in the lard, turning them with a fish-slice so that each side is slightly browned. They will take about ten minutes. When they are done, lift them out with a strainer spoon or fish-slice and drain them thoroughly of fat on a piece of soft paper. Sprinkle them with salt and serve them on a paper in a dish – the paper will absorb any fat that has not been drained away.

RECIPE 4.
Rhubarb Princess. (Cost: about 1/3½.)

2 bundles forced rhubarb	6d. worth cream
4 ozs. sugar	2 ozs. marshmallows

Buy two bundles of rhubarb – the long pink kind that is tied up in bundles of three or four sticks. Wash the sticks and cut them up into pieces about two inches long. Put the pieces with half a teacupful of water and two tablespoonfuls of castor sugar in a saucepan and stew very gently until soft. Then take the saucepan away from the fire and mash the rhubarb with the back of a wooden spoon until it is all resolved into a *purée*. Pour this into custard or grapefruit glasses, and leave to cool.

Now cut up two ounces of marshmallows – which you can buy at any sweetshop – into quarters with a pair of scissors. Put about six of these pieces into each glass. Whip up sixpennyworth of cream until it is stiff, then mix into it two tablespoonfuls of castor sugar. Pile this over the marshmallows and rhubarb.

N.B. – On no account must the rhubarb be too much sweetened. The success of this dish depends on the contrast between the sweetness of the cream and marshmallows and the tartness of the rhubarb. Be very certain, also, that the sweet is thoroughly cold. Lukewarm rhubarb has a medicinal twang and is repulsive.

SHOPPING LIST

	s.	d.
Poulterer.		
2 poussins, trussed, with giblets...	3	o
Dairy.		
Cream	o	6
Greengrocer.		
1 bundle watercress	o	1
1 lb. small tomatoes	o	5
1 lb. potatoes	o	1½
2 bundles rhubarb	o	5
Sweetshop.		
2 ozs. marshmallows	o	3½
From Stock.		
Oil	o	o½
2 ozs. lard	o	1
4 ozs. sugar	o	1
	5	o½

DINNERS FOR BEGINNERS

TIME-TABLE

Dinner at Eight O'Clock

N.B. – If you are dining at a different hour, calculate from the time-table the hour at which you will need to start your preparations and then alter the hands of the kitchen clock to conform with the time-table. You will find this easier than making individual calculations over every item.

———————

The day before, boil the potatoes to make to-day's *sauté* potatoes. In the morning, or at about 4 o'clock at the latest, prepare the rhubarb and leave it in glasses to cool.

6 30   *Wash giblets, put in salted water and start bringing to the boil.*

Lay the Table

6 45   Slice potatoes.
          Mix pepper and salt on plate.
          Put oil in cup.
          Wash and drain cress.

6 55   *Put chickens in hot water with giblets, bring gently to boil and simmer.*
          Cut up and arrange marshmallows.
          Whip cream, pile over rhubarb and marshmallows.

7 10   (about). *Take out chickens, drain and leave to cool.*
          Continue to simmer giblets.
          Light oven.
          Light grill.
          Put fireproof dish in bottom of oven to warm.

7 15   Untruss chickens, take out skewers and cut in halves.
          Rub chickens with seasoning and paint with oil.

SEVEN DINNERS FOR SPRING

7 20   *Start grilling first two halves of chicken.*
     Wipe tomatoes.
7 23   *Turn chicken.*
7 26   *Put halves of chicken in fireproof dish in bottom of oven.*
     Start grilling second two halves of chicken.
7 30   *Turn.*
7 33   *Put second two halves of chicken in fireproof dish with*
     first two halves.
7 34   Paint tomatoes with oil.
     Start grilling tomatoes.
7 37   *Turn.*
7 40   *Put tomatoes in fireproof dish with chicken.*
     Take out grilling pan, turn grill UPWARDS, put pan
     by edge of stove where fat can keep hot.

PUT PLATES AND DISHES TO WARM BENEATH GRILL OR
ON TOP OF RACK

7 43   *Start heating lard in frying-pan.*
7 45   *Start frying potatoes.*
     Start making gravy in grilling-pan.

YOU MUST KEEP ONE EYE ON THE POTATOES IN ORDER TO
TURN THEM WHEN ONE SIDE BECOMES BROWN

7 55   Put gravy in dish in bottom of oven to keep warm.
7 59   Lift out potatoes, set to drain.
     Pour fat from frying-pan into bowl or cup, wipe
     round frying-pan with paper.
8 0   Arrange chicken with tomatoes and cress on hot
     dish.
     Sprinkle potatoes with salt, put in hot dish.

If people are late, the chicken and tomatoes must remain in the fireproof dish in the oven side by side with

the gravy. The potatoes must be kept, covered, in the hot vegetable dish. None of these things will improve with keeping – particularly the potatoes. On the other hand, none will be rendered uneatable, if you take care.

CHICKEN CAROLINE

(WITH SPAGHETTI, AND A LEMON AND

MUSHROOM SAUCE)

PEAS A LA FRANCAISE

FLOATING ISLAND

(CARAMEL OF EGGS)

There comes a time in the late spring when new potatoes are still expensive and old ones have developed all sorts of undesirable traits. Try spaghetti for a change.

When eggs are plentiful, Floating Island is an inexpensive sweet.

RECIPE 1.
Chicken Caroline. (Cost: about 3/9.)

1 chicken	1½ ozs. butter
¼ lb. mushrooms	1 oz. flour
1 lemon	A few cloves
1 onion	Pepper, salt
½ lb. spaghetti	

Buy a fat little chicken for 2/9 and see that the poulterer sends the giblets. Wash these, trimming away bits of fat and skin, and put them in a saucepan of cold water with plenty of salt, pepper and an onion, which you must first peel and stick with a few cloves – poke them into the onion, it is quite easy. Heat the water slowly and while it is heating cut the chicken up into joints with a sharp knife. A demonstration is the ideal way of learning how to do this, but the following description may help.

Use a pair of scissors, to cut the skin, and a very sharp, pointed knife. Put the knife between the leg of the chicken and the side, and cut through the leg at the joint. You will find it easier, as an amateur, to do this if you cut the skin away round the joint first with scissors. The skin is quite loose and will come away easily, revealing more of the bird's anatomy.

Cut off both legs and in similar fashion cut off the wings. You have only to find the joint by exploring with your fingers outside the bird. Cut right through the gristly part between the joints.

Then make an incision just above the merry-thought, or wish-bone – again feeling for it with your fingers first if you are not sure which end it is. Turn back the merry-thought and neck bones and cut them off.

Now cut the breast away from each side of the bone, making two fillets.

When the water with the giblets in it is very hot, but not boiling, put in the jointed chicken, bring the water slowly to the boil again and simmer for twenty minutes. Then take out the pieces of chicken, drain them and leave them to cool a little. Let the giblets continue to simmer in the saucepan. When the chicken is cool enough to handle, remove carefully any skin that seems thick or rough, then put the pieces in a warm fireproof dish, cover it and put it in the bottom of a very slow oven to keep hot.

Now make *Sauce Caroline*. Wipe and peel a quarter of a pound of mushrooms and cut them into thinnish slices. If the stalks are not very coarse and old, peel these also and cut them into pieces. Heat about half an ounce of butter in a saucepan with a lid. When the butter is melted and very hot, add the mushrooms and shake the saucepan about so that they may cook a little in the butter and colour on all sides without being burnt. After about three minutes, add the juice of a lemon (strained) and pepper and salt. Close the lid and cook very gently for fifteen minutes.

While the mushrooms are cooking you must make a white sauce. Put an ounce of butter into a saucepan and when it is very hot, add a tablespoonful of sieved flour. Mix this into the butter with a wooden spoon and take the saucepan to the edge of the stove. Now add, little by little and stirring hard all the time, about half a pint of the water with the giblets simmering in it. As soon as the sauce is completely smooth, return the saucepan to the flame and bring the liquid to the boil. Continue stirring and let the sauce boil gently all over (that is to say, not just at the edge of the saucepan) for six or seven minutes. At the end of this time, the mushrooms will probably be cooked and have absorbed all the moisture in their saucepan. (If this should happen before the

73

white sauce is ready and you should hear a hissing from the mushroom saucepan, you must take the latter away from the flame and set it at the edge of the stove.) Turn all the contents of the saucepan in which the mushrooms have been cooking into the white sauce, give it a good stir round, and let it simmer for a few minutes longer, still stirring. Now taste again and see if it needs any more seasoning.

Pour this Sauce Caroline over the chickens in the fireproof dish and continue to cook in the oven at the lowest possible heat with the lid closed while you cook the peas and the spaghetti.

Spaghetti.

Put a handful of salt into a saucepan with a quart of water and bring to the boil. When it boils, add half a pound of spaghetti, broken into finger-length pieces; boil quickly for about fifteen minutes. Taste a little piece – it should be soft, but 'tacky' and not of a pasty consistency. As soon as the spaghetti is of the right consistency, pour it out and drain it in a colander, then put it in a warm dish and sprinkle it with plenty of pepper and salt.

The spaghetti can be served in a separate dish or the chicken can be put in the middle of a large dish with the spaghetti at either end. Have plenty of butter on the table, and let people mix this in with their spaghetti while it is still hot.

RECIPE 2.

Peas *à la Française.* (Cost: about 7d.)

2 lbs. peas	½ oz. butter
2 or 3 small onions	½ pint stock
Small bouquet of parsley	Pepper, salt

Shell two pounds of peas, being careful to let no worm slip past your eye, wash them and put them in a saucepan with two or three small onions, peeled, half an ounce of butter, and a breakfastcupful of the water in which the chicken and giblets have cooked. Add a spray of parsley, washed, and pepper and salt. Cover the saucepan closely and cook very gently for an hour.

To serve, remove the parsley and put the peas in a hot dish.

RECIPE 3.

Floating Island. (Cost: about 9½d.)

3 eggs	½ pint milk
4 ozs. castor sugar	2d. worth cream
2 ozs. lump sugar	2 tablespoonfuls water

Separate the yolks of three eggs from the whites by cracking each egg against the side of a bowl, then breaking it in halves and allowing the white to drip down into the bowl while you turn the yolk from one half of the shell to the other. Set the yolks aside in another bowl.

Whip the whites of egg stiffly with a fork, then fold in three tablespoonfuls of castor sugar. (Go on

75

whipping until the mixture is smooth, stiff and a pure china white. When it is really stiff it will be heavy and difficult to beat. This will probably take you about fifteen minutes and unless you are used to it it will make your wrist ache – rest your wrist from time to time, it is not necessary to beat every second of the fifteen minutes.) Leave the stiffly-whipped whites while you make a caramel.

Put two ounces of lump sugar with two table-spoonfuls of water in a saucepan and heat, stirring and watching carefully, until the mixture gets very sticky and thick and throws up a lot of bubbles, finally turning yellow and then a light brown. This will take about ten minutes. As soon as the mixture starts to turn brown, and appears to be getting very thick, pour it out into the bottom of a dry tin mould, and then turn the mould about with your hands until the inside is coated with caramel. Almost instantly the caramel will begin to set. Give the stiffly whipped whites a final beating and, as soon as the caramel lining to the mould is set, i.e., as soon as it forms a firm, toffee-like lining, pour in the whites. They must not come to the top of the mould, but should fill rather more than half of it. Tie paper over.

Set the mould to cook gently in a pan of hot water in the oven for thirty minutes. Now turn the mixture out of the mould into a glass dish. It should look like a small white cake with a brown top, and perhaps streaks of brown down the sides, and should be quite firm.

Just before serving, pour round it a rich custard made from the three yolks.

Custard.

Heat half a pint of milk with a piece of lemon peel (you will have some left over from the chicken dish) in a double-lipped saucepan. While the milk is heating, beat the three yolks for a minute with a tablespoonful of sugar, and pour them into the top of a double boiler. Heat some water in the lower half of the double boiler, *but do not let it boil*. When the milk is just about to boil, take it away from the flame, and add it gradually to the beaten yolks, stirring gently all the time. Remove the lemon peel. When all the milk is added, put the top half of the boiler over the hot water below, then turn up the flame a little and stir the custard gently until you feel it thickening under the spoon. The moment it begins to thicken, take it away from the flame and go on stirring for a minute or two. It will probably continue to thicken a little. While it is still warm, stir in twopennyworth of cream. Let the custard get thoroughly cold before you pour it round the caramel of eggs.

N.B. – If you do not constantly stir the egg while adding the milk, it may curdle, and if you let the custard heat too quickly or too long, the same thing will happen. Watch very carefully for the first sign of thickening.

DINNERS FOR BEGINNERS

SHOPPING LIST

	s.	d.
Poulterer.		
1 small chicken, with giblets	2	9
Dairy.		
½ pint milk	0	1½
Cream	0	2
3 eggs	0	4½
Greengrocer.		
¼ lb. mushrooms	0	7½
2 lbs. peas	0	6
1 lemon	0	1
Grocer.		
½ lb. Italian spaghetti	0	2
From Stock.		
2 ozs. butter (for sauce and peas)	0	2
3 or 4 small onions	0	0½
7 ozs. sugar	0	1½
Flour, cloves, parsley	negligible	
	5	1½

TIME-TABLE

DINNER AT EIGHT O'CLOCK

N.B. – If you are dining at a different time, calculate
from the time-table the hour at which you will have to
start your preparations and then alter the hands of the
kitchen clock to conform with the time-table. You will
find this easier than making individual calculations over
every item.

SEVEN DINNERS FOR SPRING

This is a strenuous dinner to cook, so don't start on it unless you are feeling strong and calm.

It would be best to make the caramel of eggs and the custard in the morning, turning out the caramel on to a dish and leaving the custard to cool in the saucepan in which it was cooked. They will take an hour to cook. If you cannot spare time to do this in the morning, then you must work in the caramel with the rest of the meal, like this. (And you will have to start early.)

5	0	LAY THE TABLE
5	10	Shell peas.
		Joint chicken.
		Wipe, peel and slice mushrooms.
		Squeeze out lemon juice.
		Wash spray of parsley.
		Peel 4 small onions, stick one with cloves.
		Wash and trim giblets.
6	0	*Start cooking giblets and onion stuck with cloves in cold salted water.*

WASH YOUR HANDS THOROUGHLY BECAUSE OF ONION

Start on the sweet. Separate yolks and whites of eggs, set yolks aside, *whip up whites and add sugar.*

6	20	*Start making caramel.*
		Light oven.
		Start heating water for bain marie (dish in which sweet is to cook).
6	30	*Coat tin mould with caramel.*
		Give whites final whipping, pour into coated mould. Tie paper over.
6	33	*Start cooking sweet in oven in baking dish of hot water.*

79

DINNERS FOR BEGINNERS

6 40 (about). *Put chicken in saucepan with giblets. Start
making custard with yolks.*

6 55 *Stir in cream. Set custard aside to cool.*

6 56 *Start cooking peas* in saucepan with butter, onions
and liquid drawn from saucepan in which
chicken is cooking. Stir, add parsley, salt, pepper.

7 02 Put fireproof dish for chicken in bottom of oven.
*Turn down oven, take out caramel and turn out into glass
dish.*

7 05 *Heat butter for mushrooms.*
Start cooking mushrooms in butter.

7 09 *Add lemon juice to mushrooms, season and simmer.*

7 10 *Take out chicken,* drain and leave to cool.
Start making white sauce.

7 25 *Add contents of mushroom pan to sauce,* stir and put at
edge of stove.
Take skin off pieces of chicken.

7 30 *Take out fireproof dish* (the one you put in at 7 02)
from oven.
Put pieces of chicken in this, stir sauce and pour over.
Close lid, put dish in oven at low heat.

7 35 *Start boiling salted water for spaghetti.*

PUT PLATES AND DISHES TO WARM IN RACK. THE DISH FOR
THE SPAGHETTI MUST GO IN THE BOTTOM OF THE OVEN

WASH UP AS MUCH AS POSSIBLE. THE MOULD IN WHICH YOU
COOKED THE CARAMEL NEEDS VERY HOT WATER

7 45 *Start boiling spaghetti.*

SEVEN DINNERS FOR SPRING

7 55   Pour custard round caramel.
8 0   *Turn out and drain spaghetti.*
       Turn out peas into hot dish.
       Place chicken on large hot dish, pile spaghetti at either
       end.

If people are late, you can leave the chicken in the oven.
Put the drained spaghetti in a hot dish with the lid on in
the plate-rack, keeping a small flame directly underneath.
Do the same with the peas.

LANCASHIRE HOTPOT

RED CABBAGE

PETITS POTS DE CREME

(JAMAICA)

Like most traditional local dishes, Lancashire hotpot has a dozen different variations. Some cooks make it with carrots, others without. One will put mutton into it, another beef, a third makes it with sausages, a fourth adds kidneys. Sometimes the hotpot turns aristocrat and includes oysters. But, whatever else it may contain, it must always have a flavour of onion and a sturdy backbone of potato (with a brown cap of potato at the top) and it must be cooked very slowly for a long time – half a day, if you dare leave it – in a deep fireproof dish. Hotpot is no aristocrat, in spite of the oysters, but an excellent and comforting dish for the freezing night that is too apt to hang over into an English spring.

Most people associate red cabbage strictly with pickles. Here it appears in proper Lancashire style as an accompaniment to the hotpot.

Petits pots de crème is a dish with a long history. The tradition is an international one this time, and only varies with the number of eggs used and the type of flavouring – you can flavour it with almost anything. Black treacle is used here because it gives an unusual and pleasant flavour, something between coffee and caramel, and because the hotpot is such an economical first course that you can afford to be reckless for once and buy a whole tin of treacle for the sake of just one tablespoonful of flavouring. Why not make real treacle toffee with the rest?

RECIPE 1.
Lancashire Hotpot. (Cost: about 2/10.)

    1¾ lbs. best end New Zealand neck of mutton
    2 sheep's kidneys
    2½ lbs. potatoes
    1½ lbs. onions
    1 carrot
    Pinch of herbs
    Salt, pepper
    1 gill water

Buy a pound and three quarters of best end of New Zealand neck of mutton and two sheep's kidneys. The best end should be all cutlets. Ask the butcher to trim these and to send you the bones and trimmings.

Mix a tablespoonful of salt with half a teaspoonful of pepper on a plate. Skin, split and core the kidneys with a sharp knife, then rub them with the mixed seasoning and cut them into thin slices. Cut the meat of the cutlets carefully from the bones; cut each one into pieces about an inch square and rub these also with the seasoning.

Now make some *stock*. Cut any fat from the mutton

trimmings and set it aside to be slowly rendered down into dripping in the oven. If you don't want to do this, then throw the fat away. Wash the bones and meaty parts of the trimmings in cold water, and put them together with the cutlet bones, also washed, in a saucepan. Add a dessertspoonful of salt, a good sprinkling of pepper, an onion peeled and quartered, some parsley if you have it handy, and a good pinch of herbs tied up in muslin. Cover well with cold water and set the saucepan over a low heat with the lid nearly closed, to come slowly to the boil. When it boils, let it just simmer for an hour, or as long as you can give it – the longer the better. Keep the heat always very low, and add fresh hot water if the stock gets low. It may appear a little scummy on first boiling, but should become almost clear after long simmering. This stock is not wanted for the hotpot itself, but for the red cabbage. It should be made early, however, and you must put it on to cook before you go ahead with the hotpot, which continues thus:

Peel and slice a pound or a little more of onions. Peel two and a half pounds of potatoes and cut them into slices about an eighth of an inch thick; dry these in a cloth. Wash and scrape a carrot and cut it into rings of about the thickness of a florin. Now take a round or oval fireproof dish that is really deep and large. Put a thick layer of sliced potatoes in the bottom; sprinkle them with pepper and salt. Next put a layer of onion, mutton and kidney (which you have flavoured before starting on the stock) and carrot, mixed. Repeat these two layers until the dish is full; make the top layer a good thick one of potatoes. Sprinkle over a teacupful of water.

Cover with greaseproof paper and cook in the oven at low heat for as long as possible – not less than three hours, with an extra three quarters of an hour at the end, when the paper is taken off and the potatoes are allowed to brown at the top – let them get quite dark and crisp. In Lancashire this dish is sometimes put on early in the morning for a meal at six o'clock, and it is all the better for it. It can safely be left to cook itself.

Serve in the dish in which it was cooked with a clean napkin folded and pinned round it. There is no real need for the napkin if you are using a modern fireproof dish – it is just a gesture to tradition.

RECIPE 2.
Red Cabbage. (Cost: about 8½d.)

1 red cabbage	1 gill stock
1 onion	I dessertspoonful wine vine-
Salt, pepper	gar
1 teaspoonful castor sugar	2 rashers fat, streaky bacon

Buy a good-sized red cabbage and cut off and throw away any discoloured or damaged outer leaves. Cut it in quarters, remove any stalk, shred it up finely and wash it under cold, running water. Now drain it and cook it for five minutes in boiling salted water with the lid of the saucepan off. After five minutes, drain the cabbage and put it into a fireproof dish with a teacupful of the stock which you made from the bones and trimmings of the mutton, a dessertspoonful of wine vinegar, a teaspoonful of castor sugar, a small onion peeled and cut in halves and one or two rashers of fat streaky bacon cut into very small pieces. Add a good sprinkling of pepper, but no salt, and stir all together. Do not cover, and cook slowly on the shelf below the hotpot for an hour.

Serve in the dish in which it was cooked, first removing the onion.

N.B. – Other kinds of cabbage are delicious cooked in the same way.

RECIPE 3.
Petits Pots de Crème (Jamaica). (Cost: about 1/5.)

6 eggs	1 pint milk
2 ozs. castor sugar	Small tin black Jamaica treacle

Put a pint of milk in a saucepan with two tablespoonfuls of castor sugar and a tablespoonful of black treacle. Heat gently, stirring with a wooden spoon all the time, until the milk boils. Then let it get cold. It will take about five minutes, or less, to boil, and fifteen minutes to cool.

When the milk is cold, separate the yolks of five eggs from the whites by cracking each egg against the edge of a bowl and breaking it in half, allowing the white to drip down into the bowl while you turn the yolk from one half of the shell to the other. Put the whites aside and add one whole egg, white and yolk, to the yolks. Beat these with a fork for half a minute.

Strain the flavoured milk on to the eggs and mix all thoroughly, but gently, with the wooden spoon. Pass the mixture through a fine hair sieve into a large bowl, and from here pour it (this will be done most easily via a pint measure with a lip) into as many little earthenware pots or small *soufflé* dishes as it will fill. Set these in a baking dish half full of hot water to cook in the oven uncovered (*au bain marie*) at a fairly low heat until the mixture is set. This will take from twenty to thirty minutes. The mixture in each pot should be quite firm in the centre as well as at the edges.

Serve hot or cold in the little pots. You will need no cream for this sweet, which should be meltingly soft and delicate in itself.

Some people may call six eggs extravagant. But it is really worth while using that number for the sake of the result. Use the whites that are left over to make one of various dishes next day – e.g., meringues (recipe for meringue crust on page 117) or apple snow (recipe on page 247).

DINNERS FOR BEGINNERS

SHOPPING LIST

		s.	d.
Butcher.			
1¾ lbs. best end of New Zealand mutton (all cutlets) (to be trimmed, and trimmings sent)		1	9
2 sheep's kidneys		0	6
Dairy.			
1 pint milk		0	3
6 eggs		0	9
Greengrocer.			
2½ lbs. potatoes		0	4
2 lbs. onions (for hotpot, stock and cabbage)		0	3
1 red cabbage		0	6
Grocer.			
1 small tin Jamaica treacle		0	4½
From Stock.			
1 carrot		0	0½
2 rashers bacon		0	2
2½ ozs. castor sugar (for cabbage and sweet) ...		0	0½
Vinegar, herbs, negligible, or at most		0	0½
		5	**0**

TIME-TABLE

DINNER AT EIGHT O'CLOCK

N.B. – If you are dining at a different time, calculate from the time-table the hour at which you will have to start your preparations and then alter the hands of the kitchen clock to conform with the time-table. You will find this easier than making individual calculations over every item.

———

Unless you can start on this dinner very early – at about 3.30 – you had better start cooking the stock and hotpot in the morning or on the evening before.

It will take you a quarter of an hour or twenty minutes to prepare and season the mutton and kidneys and start the stock, and at least a further twenty minutes to peel and cut up the vegetables for the hotpot. Allow yourself three-quarters of an hour for everything, and then give the hotpot and stock a preliminary cooking of two hours. Half the battle will now be over, and you have an easy meal to cook. (¾-hour plus 2 hours—2¾ hours.)

6 0 *Light oven.*
       Start simmering stock.

LAY THE TABLE

6 10 *Put hotpot in very slow oven, at the top.*
        Start making sweet: boil flavoured milk and allow
           to cool.
6 30 *Start heating water for bain marie.*
        Separate yolks and whites. Beat yolks with one
           white.
        Mix with flavoured milk, pass through sieve and
           pour into pots.
6 40 *Start boiling salted water for cabbage.*
        Turn up oven slightly, move hotpot to lower shelf.
        Pour hot water into baking dish, stand pots in this
           (bain marie), and *start cooking on top shelf of oven.*
        Cut up cabbage, wash and drain.
6 50 *Start boiling cabbage.*
        Peel and halve onion.
        Cut rind off rashers of bacon, chop small.

6 55   *Drain cabbage.*
Draw off teacupful of water from stock.
Put cabbage in fireproof dish with onion, bacon,
stock, vinegar, sugar, pepper.

7 0   *If sweet is set, remove it from oven, turn heat down to*
very low, put hotpot on top shelf and cabbage on shelf
below.
If sweet is not yet set, just put cabbage on shelf below
hotpot.
WHENEVER YOU DO REMOVE THE SWEET, TURN
DOWN THE OVEN HEAT TO VERY LOW AND MOVE
THE HOTPOT AND CABBAGE EACH ONE SHELF
HIGHER

7 15   *Take paper off hotpot.*
YOU HAVE NOW NOTHING MORE TO DO EXCEPT
TO DRY THE LITTLE POTS AND ARRANGE THEM ON A
TRAY, TO PUT THE PLATES TO WARM IN THE
BOTTOM OF THE OVEN AND TO PIN THE NAPKIN
ROUND THE HOTPOT
PUT THE PLATES IN AT 7.45

If people are late, leave everything as it is, unless the top
of the hotpot is burning, in which case you must cover it
again.

SAVOURY PORK CHOPS

APPLE SAUCE

BRAISED SEAKALE

MASHED POTATOES

APRICOT PUREE

This is a very simple meal to cook and is a good choice for a beginner, more especially as it need not be served the moment it is cooked, but can wait quite happily in the oven for some little time.

RECIPE 1.
Savoury Pork Chops. (Cost: about 2/1½.)

4 pork chops	Teaspoonful tarragon vinegar
1 lb. Spanish onions	A little French mustard
Pepper, salt	½ teaspoonful dried sage

Trim most of the fat off your chops, wipe them and rub them all over on both sides with a little tarragon vinegar. After this, rub a little French mustard into them.

Peel and quarter a pound of Spanish onions and put them into a saucepan of boiling, salted water. Boil rapidly for about fifteen minutes with the lid off. At the end of this time the onions will still be hard, but turn them out into a colander and drain them well. Chop them up fairly fine, add pepper and

91

salt and mix into them about half a teaspoonful of dried sage.

Line a large flat fireproof dish with the onion mixture, reserving some to spread over the chops. Place the chops on the bed of onion and cover them with the remainder of the onion. Bake uncovered in a hot oven for about fifty minutes or a little longer.

RECIPE 2.

Apple Sauce. (Cost: about 4½d.)

    1 lb. soft cooking apples   ½ oz. butter
    2 ozs. sugar

Buy a pound of cooking apples, which must not be of a hard type. Peel, quarter and core them, then cut them into slices. Put them in a small saucepan with a very little cold water – about two table-spoonfuls – and two tablespoonfuls of white sugar. Bring them to simmering-point, stirring all the time with a wooden spoon, and simmer them very gently for about fifteen minutes. The apples must be re-duced by cooking and stirring to a smooth pulp. After fifteen minutes, stir about a dessertspoonful of butter into the hot apples and, if its handle will permit, put the saucepan into the oven and leave it there for eight or ten minutes – the sauce can, alter-natively, finish cooking on the top of the stove, but as you are using the oven for other dishes, your last-minute cooking will be easier if you have everything together in the oven.

This sauce can be cooked entirely in the oven, in

which case the apples would take longer to cook – at least forty-five minutes.

RECIPE 3.

Braised Seakale. (Cost: about 11d.)

1 lb. seakale	1 oz. butter
Teaspoonful vinegar	Pepper, salt

Trim the roots of the seakale and wash it carefully under the tap. Be sure to free it completely from grit. Have ready a saucepan of boiling, salted water, large enough to take the seakale lying down. Tie the seakale in a bundle with cotton or string (this makes it easier to lift out of the water without damaging it) and put it into the boiling water, together with a teaspoonful of vinegar. Boil, fairly quickly, with the lid off, for five minutes, then lift out the seakale, drain it, untie it and put it in a fireproof dish with pepper, a sprinkling of salt and an ounce of butter. Put the lid on the dish and hold well down while you toss the seakale round – the butter will melt on touching the hot seakale and will be distributed evenly over it. Keep the lid on and cook in the oven at low heat for from forty-five minutes to an hour.

RECIPE 4.

Mashed Potatoes. (Cost: about 2½d.)

1½ lbs. old potatoes	2 tablespoonfuls milk
½ oz. butter	Salt, pepper, paprika

Peel a pound and a half of old potatoes, cutting them into approximately equal sizes so that all may

93

be cooked at the same time. Put them in a saucepan with plenty of salt and cold water to cover them and cook for about twenty-five minutes with the lid almost closed. Then test with a knitting-needle to see if they are cooked. They should be soft, but not breaking.

Drain the potatoes in the colander, dry the saucepan and return the potatoes to it, setting it by the edge of the flame. Cover with a dry cloth, which will absorb the moisture from the potatoes. As soon as they are dry, take a fork and mash them in the saucepan, adding pepper, salt, a slice of butter and about two tablespoonfuls of milk. You must keep on mashing until the potato *purée* is smooth and white with not a lump or a grey bit in it anywhere. Turn into a hot vegetable dish and sprinkle with paprika.

RECIPE 5.
Apricot *Purée*. (Cost: about 1/4½.)

1 lb. evaporated apricots	6d. worth of cream
1 small tin apricots	1 tablespoonful sugar

Soak a pound of evaporated apricots in plenty of cold water over-night. To cook, put the apricots in a saucepan with about a teacupful of cold water, bring gently to simmering-point and simmer for about twenty minutes. Then add all the contents of a small tin of apricots to the saucepan and continue to simmer until the syrup surrounding the apricots is considerably reduced – this will take about fifteen minutes. Stir in a tablespoonful of white sugar with the tin of apricots.

When cooked, pass through a wire sieve, using a wooden spoon, mashing to and fro across the centre of the sieve and being careful to look at the under side of the sieve where a lot of the *purée* will be hanging. Pour the *purée* into a glass dish and let it get cold. Just before serving, whip up sixpenny-worth of cream until it is just beginning to stiffen and pour it over the *purée* – or, if the latter is very liquid, send round the partly-whipped cream in a separate bowl and scatter some chopped pistachio nuts over the apricot *purée*.

SHOPPING LIST

						s.	d.
Butcher.							
4 pork chops	...	...	...	...	...	2	0
Dairy.							
Cream	...	...	...	...	...	0	6
Greengrocer.							
1 lb. Spanish onions	...	...	...	...	0	1½
1 lb. soft cooking apples		...	...	...	0	3
1 lb. seakale	...	...	...	...	...	0	10
1½ lbs. old potatoes	...	...	...	...	0	2
Grocer.							
1 lb. evaporated apricots (day before)			...	0	6
1 small tin apricots	...	...	...	...	0	4½
From Stock.							
2½ ozs. butter	...	...	...	...	...	0	2½
3 ozs. sugar	...	...	...	...	...	0	0½
Vinegar, French mustard, sage, paprika, milk, pistachio nuts, negligible, or at most			...	0	0½
						5	0½

DINNERS FOR BEGINNERS

TIME-TABLE

Dinner at Eight O'Clock

N.B. – If you are dining at a different time, calculate from the time-table at what hour you will have to start your preparations and then alter the hands of the kitchen clock to conform with the time-table. You will find this easier than making individual calculations over every item.

Overnight. Soak apricots in basin with plenty of water.
Make the apricot *purée* in the morning or by six o'clock at the latest, unless the weather is very cold.

6	0	**LAY THE TABLE**
6	15	*Start boiling salted water for onions.*
		Peel onions.
		Wash and trim seakale, tie it up.
6	25	*Start boiling onions,*
		Trim and prepare chops.
		Peel, core and quarter apples. Slice them thinly.
6	40	*Drain onions. Chop, season, add sage.*
		Arrange chops and onions in fireproof dish.
6	45	*Start boiling salted water for seakale.*
		Light oven.
6	55	*Put seakale in boiling water with vinegar.*
7	0	*Start cooking chops in oven.*
		Drain seakale, put in dish with seasoning and butter.
		Start cooking seakale.
7	5	*Start cooking apples.*
		Peel and prepare potatoes, leave in water.
7	20	*Pulp apples with wooden spoon and set saucepan at edge of stove.*

7 25   *Start cooking potatoes* in cold salted water.

PUT PLATES AND DISHES TO WARM IN BOTTOM OF
OVEN OR ON RACK ABOVE POTATOES
YOU HAVE A LITTLE INTERVAL HERE

7 45   *Stir butter into apples and set in warm place.*

7 47   Partly whip cream and arrange on apricots or in
separate dish.

7 50   *Drain potatoes, dry in saucepan and mash* with butter,
milk and seasoning.

Put potato *purée* in hot vegetable dish.

Put apple sauce in hot gravy dish.

(Chops and seakale are served in the dishes in
which they were cooked.)

If people are late, the chops, seakale and apple sauce can
all be left in their dishes in the oven, with the heat turned
down very low. The potatoes can be covered and left in
the saucepan in which they were mashed.

Do not sprinkle paprika over the potatoes or pour the
cream over the apricot *purée* until the last moment.

WATERCRESS SOUP

BAKED LEMON SOLE

ITALIAN RICE

GOLDEN PUDDING

RECIPE 1.

Watercress Soup. (Cost: about 5½d.)

1 bunch watercress	1 oz. butter
1 egg	½ oz. rice
½ bunch parsley	

Wash a 2d. bunch of fine healthy-looking watercress, pick the leaves off the stems and drop them into boiling salted water for a minute. Turn them into a colander, drain them well, and then put the leaves on a board and chop them. (They will look very small, but never mind.) Put a small piece of butter in a saucepan and heat it. When it sizzles, drop in the watercress and fry it for a few seconds, turning it about with a wooden spoon. Then add enough hot water to make the soup – about two pints, for four people.

Add salt and pepper and, if you happen to have it, part of the green leaves of a head of celery, chopped. Throw in a small handful of rice.

Bring very slowly to the boil and simmer for half an hour.

Wash and chop some parsley and add it to the soup. Simmer for another quarter of an hour.

Now separate the yolk from the white of an egg by cracking the egg against the side of a basin and allowing the white to drip down into the basin while you turn the yolk from one half of the shell to the other.

Beat the yolk, and place it in a large bowl or tureen. Add a small lump of butter.

Pour the soup on the yolk and butter, stir gently, but thoroughly. The soup is ready, but can be returned to the pan if necessary and kept warm by the side of the fire. Remove any celery before serving.

RECIPE 2.
Baked Lemon Sole. (Cost: about 2/10.)

2 lbs. fillet lemon sole	A little butter
Bay leaf	1 Lemon
Pepper, salt	

Ask the fishmonger to fillet and skin the soles, making sure that he removes *all* the skin. Lay the fillets out, sprinkle them with salt, pepper and a little lemon juice, and roll them loosely.

Put a bay leaf in the bottom of a fireproof dish, and then put in the sole. Put a little piece of butter on the top of each roll, and pour over all two tablespoonfuls of strained lemon juice. Cover with a piece of greaseproof paper, and cook in a slow oven for twenty-five minutes. Remove the bay leaf, and serve the fish on the same dish as the rice, or separately, whichever you prefer.

99

RECIPE 3.

Italian Rice. (Cost: about 8d.)

| ¼ lb. rice | 1 small tin tomatoes |
| 2 ozs. butter | 3 or 4 shallots |

Peel and chop very finely three or four shallots. Open the tin of tomatoes. Melt two ounces of butter in a frying-pan, and when it is frothing, turn into it a teacupful of rice. It will disappear beneath the froth of butter. Stir with a wooden spoon continuously for five minutes, during which time the rice will gradually appear larger in bulk, and turn a pale brown.

Take the pan to the side of the fire, and add the contents of the tin of tomatoes, and the chopped shallots. Stir well, and season.

Cover the frying-pan with an enamel plate, and simmer for thirty minutes, by which time the rice will be quite soft and will have absorbed all the moisture.

Serve on the same dish as the fish, or separately, whichever you prefer.

RECIPE 4.

Golden Pudding. (Cost: about 9d.)

4 ozs. butter	4 ozs. sugar
4 ozs. flour	4 ozs. golden syrup
2 eggs	1 tablespoonful water
½ teaspoonful baking powder	

Put four ounces of golden syrup in a basin. This is a quarter of a pound-tin, and in this case it is perfectly permissible to guess the quantity from the tin.

But if you want to weigh or measure it exactly, flour the pan of the scales lightly and evenly and pour the syrup on to this. It will slip off, leaving the pan quite clean. Or flour a tablespoon and extract four spoonfuls of the syrup from the tin.

Add to the syrup one tablespoonful of water, and mix it well until the syrup is evenly diluted to a thinner consistency. Then pour it into the bottom of the *well-greased* fireproof dish in which the pudding is to be cooked. (Do not do the mixing of syrup and water in this dish, as the syrup is then bound to smear the sides a little.)

Now put ¼ lb. butter in a mixing bowl and cream it with a wooden spoon – that is, smash it about until it is of a consistency which it would be just possible to stir. Then add ¼ lb. castor sugar and continue to cream the two together. When they are perfectly smooth, beat up the two eggs well, and add them to the butter and sugar. Stir well until the mixture is stiff and uniform. Now sift the flour and baking powder together and add them to the mixture. Blend well. The mixture will now be just too stiff to pour, but not dry enough to handle.

Turn this into the fireproof dish on top of the treacle and water, and cover it with a greased paper. Cook it in a slow to moderate oven for one hour. Do not open the oven if you can help it during this time, although in this menu it will not hurt to open it at half-time to put in the fish.

When it is cooked it will have risen considerably

and be golden in colour. Take off the paper, run a knife round the side of the pudding, and turn it out on to a hot dish. The syrup will form a thick coating on top of the pudding, and will trickle very slightly down the sides.

SHOPPING LIST

Fishmonger.   s.   d.

   2 lbs. fillet lemon sole   2   8

Dairy.

   ½ lb. butter   0   6

   3 eggs   0   4½

Greengrocer.

   1 lemon   0   1½

   1 bunch watercress   0   2

   1 bunch parsley   0   1

Grocer.

   1 small tin tomatoes   0   5½

From Stock.

   4 ozs. sugar   0   1

   4 ozs. flour   0   0½

   4 ozs. golden syrup   0   1⅓

   5 ozs. rice   0   1½

   3 or 4 shallots   0   1½

   Bay leaf, baking powder   ...   ...   negligible

                                           4   10½

SEVEN DINNERS FOR SPRING

TIME-TABLE

DINNER AT EIGHT O'CLOCK

N.B. – If you are dining at a different time, calculate from the time-table the hour at which you will have to start your preparations and then alter the hands of the kitchen clock to conform with the time-table. You will find it easier than making individual calculations over every item.

---

6 30   Wash, scald and chop watercress.
6 40   *Start to make pudding.*
        Light oven for pudding.
6 45   *Finish making pudding.*
7 0   *Put pudding in oven.*
        Melt butter for watercress.
        Fry watercress.
7 5   Add water to watercress for soup, with salt, pepper,
        etc., and *bring slowly to boil.*
                    LAY TABLE
7 20   Prepare fish.
            PUT PLATES AND DISHES TO WARM IN RACK
7 25   *Melt butter for rice.*
        Sauté rice for five minutes.
7 30   *Add tomatoes to rice, cover and leave to simmer.*
7 35   *Put fish in oven.*
        Chop parsley.
7 40   *Add parsley to soup.*
7 55   Put yolk of egg in tureen with butter.
        Add soup and stir.
8 0   Dish rice. Take fish out of oven.
        (Turn out pudding just before serving.)

If people are late, return the soup to the pan and keep at the side of the fire. Turn heat very low in the oven and keep fish, rice and pudding covered.

CHAPTER IV

SEVEN DINNERS FOR SUMMER

Summer Menu No. 1   FOR FOUR PEOPLE

VEAL EMMA
(Cooked in Rolls, with Onion and Cabbage)
SCALLOPED POTATOES

ICED GOOSEBERRY FOOL
CAT'S TONGUE BISCUITS

RECIPE 1.

Veal Emma. (Cost: about 2/8½.)

1 lb. fillet of veal	1 oz. flour
1 cabbage	1½ ozs. butter
1 onion	Salt, pepper
Some string	A little water

A SK the butcher to cut you about a pound of fillet of English veal as THINLY AS POSSIBLE. Keep urging him to cut it thinly and ask him, further, to cut it into about eight little strips, long rather than wide. Trim away any fat and skin from these strips yourself, using a very sharp knife. Wipe the meat.

Shred off the outer leaves of a large cabbage, cut it in quarters and cut away the centre stalk. Soak the cabbage in cold, salted water until needed. Cook it for five minutes in plenty of boiling salted water, with the lid of the saucepan off. Turn out, drain and cool. Meanwhile, mix a tablespoonful of flour with a teaspoonful of salt and a good pinch of pepper on a plate. Peel an onion and cut it into thin, fairy-like slices.

As soon as the cabbage leaves are cool enough to handle, lay a slice of onion on each strip of veal and a piece of cabbage on top of the onion. Sprinkle with a very little pepper and salt, then roll each strip of veal round firmly on itself, so that it forms a kind of little pillow, and tie it securely with a piece of string or cotton. Roll each pillow, when it is tied, in the seasoned flour.

Heat an ounce and a half of butter in a saucepan. When the butter is melted and very hot, put the rolls of veal into it and sear them on both sides, moving the saucepan about so that they do not stick to the bottom. Add any pieces of veal that were too small to make into rolls. When all the veal is nicely browned – this will take about three minutes – add all the rest of the cabbage and pour in two table-spoonfuls of water (or stock, of course, if you have it) – not more. Cover the pan closely, pressing down the lid over a piece of greaseproof paper, and simmer at very low heat for an hour and a half – a simmering flame is a perfect boon for this dish, if you have one on your oven.

If at any time there should arise a smell of burning, you must add a very little more water to the veal.

Don't be agitated by this smell, but deal with it promptly. A few seconds of burning will only help to darken the gravy at the bottom of the pan and turn the veal a richer colour. It must not continue, however, or the dish will be spoilt.

To serve, lift out the pieces of veal and cut the string which ties them. TAKE CARE, they will be very hot. The veal should be a dark brown colour and look almost burnt. Lift out the cabbage, make a bed of it on a hot dish, seat the rolls of veal on the cabbage and pour over any liquid from the pan.

RECIPE 2.
Scalloped Potatoes. (Cost: about 3½d.)

> 1 lb. old potatoes   1 oz. butter
> A little over a gill of milk   Pepper, salt
> Slices of onion

Wash and peel a pound of old potatoes and cut them into slices about an eighth of an inch thick. Dry in a cloth. Butter a fireproof dish. Put in a layer of sliced potatoes. Sprinkle with pepper and salt, add any slices of onion left over from the veal and dot with tiny pieces of butter. Repeat this until the dish is more or less full and you have used up all your potato slices. Pour in some milk at the side of the dish until you can just see it through the top layer of potatoes – this will take about a gill and a half.

Bake in a moderate oven for an hour and a half. The potatoes should be quite soft and decidedly brown on top. If you don't like them browned, then cover them with greaseproof paper while they are being cooked. Serve in the dish in which they were cooked.

RECIPE 3.
Iced Gooseberry Fool. (Cost: about 1/4 – biscuits, 7½d.)

    2 lbs. gooseberries   6d. worth cream
    4 ozs. white sugar   3d. worth ice
    ¼ lb. Cat's Tongue biscuits

Buy threepennyworth of ice from the fishmonger and put it in a large bowl. Wash, top and tail two pounds of gooseberries. (They may be sold by the pint; in this case, buy two pints.) Topping and tailing means cutting off the stalks and little black remainders of flower at the top of the fruit.

Put the gooseberries in a saucepan with a quarter of a pound of white sugar and about half a gill of water. Bring to the boil, stirring with a wooden spoon, and simmer for about seven minutes. Squash the gooseberries well with the spoon.

Now put a sieve over a large basin and turn out the stewed gooseberries on to the sieve. Pass them through the sieve with the spoon. This is hard work; you must keep on squashing and scraping with the back of the spoon until as much of the gooseberries as possible is passed through into the basin below. Remember to look at the underneath of the sieve where a lot of the *purée* will be clinging.

Stir the sieved gooseberries, taste them and sweeten again if necessary. Leave to cool. When the

107

purée is cool, whip up sixpennyworth of cream until it just runs in a thick ribbon from the end of the fork; then stir it well into the *purée*. Pour this fool into the dish in which you mean to serve it and perch the dish on top of the ice – or, alternatively, smash up the ice with a hammer and arrange it round the dish. Remember to wipe the dish when you take it off the ice.

Among economical recipes this one may seem extravagant in its use of ice. But tepid gooseberry fool is insipid stuff; comparatively few people possess refrigerators or ice-boxes and for those who have neither threepennyworth of ice is always a good investment on a hot summer's day. As for the cream – gooseberry fool made with custard is certainly more economical, but it is at the same time far less nice.

With the fool hand round a quarter of a pound of Cat's Tongue biscuits, which are sold at most good baker's shops, generally for about two-and-sixpence a pound.

SEVEN DINNERS FOR SUMMER

SHOPPING LIST

	s.	d.
Butcher.		
1 lb. of fillet of English veal	2	4
Fishmonger.		
Ice	0	3
Dairy.		
Cream	0	6
Baker.		
¼ lb. Cat's Tongue biscuits	0	7½
Greengrocer.		
1 large cabbage	0	3
1 lb. potatoes	0	1½
2 lbs. (or pints) green gooseberries	0	6
(Don't buy large yellow or red hairy ones.)		
From Stock.		
1 large onion	0	1½
2½ ozs. butter	0	2
Milk (a gill and a half)	0	1
4 or 6 ozs. white sugar	0	1
	5	0½

Flour, negligible.

TIME-TABLE

DINNER AT EIGHT O'CLOCK

N.B. – If you are dining at a different time, calculate from the time-table the hour at which you will have to start your preparations and then alter the hands of the

kitchen clock to conform with the time-table. You will find this easier than making individual calculations over every item.

———

Prepare the gooseberry fool beforehand. It will take about three-quarters of an hour to prepare, and should then be left on the ice for at least two hours.

5 50 Prepare scalloped potatoes for cooking.
6 0 *Start boiling salted water for cabbage.*
      Prepare cabbage.
      Peel and slice onion.
      Prepare seasoned flour on plate.
6 10 *Start boiling cabbage.*
      Cut lengths of string or cotton for tying veal.
6 15 *Drain cabbage*, separate leaves, leave to cool.
      Prepare veal for cooking.
6 20 *Light oven for potatoes.*
6 25 Roll cabbage and onion inside veal strips, tie with
         string.
      Roll veal strips in seasoned flour.
6 30 *Start cooking veal in closed saucepan.*
      Start cooking potatoes in oven.
         WASH UP. LAY THE TABLE.
      YOU CAN NOW LEAVE THE DINNER TO COOK ITSELF.
      ONLY – DON'T FORGET TO WARM DISHES AND
      PLATES (PUT THESE IN THE BOTTOM OF THE OVEN
         AT ABOUT 7.40), AND DON'T LET THE VEAL BURN
7 40 Warm plates and dishes in bottom of oven.

If people are late, turn down the oven heat as low as possible and leave the potatoes where they are; cover them if they burn too much. Leave the veal in the saucepan at the edge of the flame.

GUINEA-FOWL A LA MERE DOUB
(Stuffed with Olives, with a Sour Cream Sauce)
GOLDEN POTATOES
PEAS

PLUM MERINGUE

There is a succulent way of cooking guinea-fowl.
Try it in the later summer months when small
purple English plums provide a very cheap sweet to
follow. The cheaper the plums, the more lavish
you can be with your cream in the sauce for the
guinea-fowl.

RECIPE 1.
Guinea-fowl *à la Mère Doub.* (Cost: about 3/11½.)

Guinea-fowl	4d. worth sour cream
¼ lb. butter	9 olives
Pepper, salt	1 to 2 tablepoonfuls of
1 egg	crumbs

Choose a plump guinea-fowl costing 3/-. The
poulterer will sell it to you trussed and with two
strips of larding bacon tied across its breast with
string; untie the string or cut it, disarranging the
bacon as little as possible, and you will discover a

cavity at one end of the bird where you can loosen the skin and free it sufficiently with a sharp knife to turn it back like a flap. (If this does not make things clear to you, ask your poulterer to explain to you where one stuffs birds.) Fill the cavity with the following mixture:

Olive Stuffing.

Buy nine olives. They are sold at three for 1d. at the delicatessen shops which sell cold meat, salads, etc. If they are very salt, leave them in cold water for an hour or two. Dry them, pare all the flesh from the stones and throw these away. Chop the flesh and mix it with one to two tablespoonfuls of white crumbs, according to the size of the bird to be stuffed. You can obtain the crumbs, if you have no really stale bread, by drying a few slices in a slow oven until they can be rubbed through the bottom of the colander or, more finely still, through a sieve.

Crack an egg against the edge of a cup and let the white drip down into the cup while you turn the yolk from one half of the shell to the other. Beat the yolk a little and add it to the olives and bread-crumbs, mixing well, so that the whole forms a fairly solid ball. Taste and add pepper – and salt if necessary. Now insert the ball of stuffing between the flesh and skin of the guinea-fowl – bit by bit if it breaks into pieces – and draw down the skin over it. See that the larding bacon is in position and tie up the bird again, making certain that the flap is securely lashed down over the stuffing – if you are not sure of this, you had better sew the flap down with needle and cotton.

STUFFING ALWAYS SEEMS A FORMIDABLE OPERATION UNTIL ONE COMES TO DO IT. IN FACT, IT IS MUCH EASIER THAN MAKING A WHITE SAUCE, AND THE RESULTS ARE ALWAYS REWARDING.

Make the oven very hot. Put the stuffed guinea-fowl into a roasting-pan – the kind with a lid, *but do not put the lid on at first* – together with a quarter of a pound of butter and a piece of greased paper folded over the breast of the bird. Put the pan in the oven and leave the heat very high for twelve to fifteen minutes, long enough, in fact, for the butter to melt and for you to baste the bird with it a few times. (Basting means pouring the hot melted fat over the bird with a spoon – you will need a long one.) The intense heat at first seals the outside of the meat so that its juices are retained underneath. If you have made your oven too hot there will be a smell of burning fat, and you must lower the heat.

After fifteen minutes, lower to a little above medium heat, put on the lid of the roaster (see that it is tightly closed) and leave the bird without any further basting for thirty minutes. Then lower the heat again until it is fairly low, but not VERY low, and cook for a last fifteen minutes.

(Fifteen, plus thirty, plus fifteen—one hour to cook in oven.)

To make the *cream sauce*, take out the guinea-fowl from the oven, cut the string and withdraw the strips of larding bacon and the wooden skewer to which the bird is fastened when it is trussed. Put the bird on a large warm dish, cover it as much as possible with the lid of the roasting-pan, turn down the oven to the lowest possible heat, and put the dish into the oven – if the oven door will not close, never mind.

Now put the roasting-pan, with the cooked butter in the bottom of it, to heat over a low flame on top of the stove. When the butter spits and sizzles, add fourpennyworth of sour cream and stir it well with the butter for three or four minutes. Taste and add plenty of salt and pepper. Serve the sauce separately.

To make *sour cream*: either buy the cream the day before and leave it in a warm place, or add a few drops of lemon juice or vinegar to the fresh cream. The very thick top part of sour unskimmed milk might serve your purpose if you have no cream.

RECIPE 2.
Golden Potatoes. (Cost: about 1½d., excluding two yolks of egg, over from the meringue.)

Wash and peel a pound of potatoes and cut them into slices about a quarter of an inch thick. Boil them in salted water until they are soft – from ten to fifteen minutes. Drain them, and return the potatoes to the saucepan by the side of the flame for a minute or two while you heat a very little milk. Add this, with a slice of butter to the dried potatoes and mash until they are absolutely smooth, NOT A LUMP LEFT.

Season with pepper and salt. Crack two eggs against a cup. Let the whites drip out, turn the yolks from one half of the shell to the other until they are free of white. Beat the yolks for a minute and mix them well with the potatoes.

Put in a greased fireproof dish and cook in the oven for the last fifteen minutes, during which the guinea-fowl is cooking. The potatoes should be a golden-yellow colour.

RECIPE 3.
Garden Peas. (Cost: about 4d.)

| 2 lbs. peas | Teaspoonful of castor sugar |
| A sprig of mint | Salt, pepper, butter |

Shell two pounds of peas and put them into boiling salted water with a little mint and a teaspoonful of castor sugar. Boil fast in a saucepan without the lid; after about fifteen minutes they will be cooked, but after they have been boiling for about twelve minutes, the cook should begin dipping in a spoon or fork and bringing out a pea or two to taste. The moment the peas are done they should be turned out of the saucepan and drained, the mint removed, and the drained peas put into a hot vegetable dish with a thin slice of butter and some pepper and salt. See that no draggled ends of mint intrude upon the dish.

It is very important that peas should not be cooked a moment too long, and it is only by constant testing that the exact moment for taking them off the fire can be ascertained. Once they are cooked and drained, however, they can be kept for a short time in the vegetable dish without coming to harm.

Serve the peas either in the vegetable dish or in two heaps, one at either end of the dish which holds the guinea-fowl.

RECIPE 4.
Plum Meringue. (Cost: about 7d. excluding one white of egg, over from stuffing.)

 1½ lbs. plums
 6 ozs. sugar
 3 whites of egg

Buy a pound and a half of the little purple plums that make their appearance in the shops soon after midsummer. Wash them, take off any stalks. Put four tablespoonfuls of castor sugar in about half an inch of water in a saucepan and bring to the boil, stirring. When the water boils, put in the plums and simmer for ten minutes or until they are all so soft that they are coming away from the stones. Turn the plums about with a wooden spoon so that they are all equally cooked.

Allow the plums to cool. This will take some time in hot weather, and can be hastened by turning the plums out into the shallowest dish you can find and putting it either in a draught or with the bottom of the dish standing in cold water. With the spoon and a fork, separate the stones from the plums and throw the stones away. This moving and stirring about will help to cool the plums. Don't take out the skins. When quite cool, give a final stir and turn into a *soufflé* dish, pouring away any superfluous water. The mixture should be THICK.

Now make the *meringue mixture* to go on top of the plums. You are using three yolks of eggs in other dishes in this meal, and have separated these from the whites, which you must now beat with a fork or whisk. Go on beating until the mixture is absolutely smooth and thick, china white in colour and looking like very pure white whipped cream. This beating will take anything from ten to fifteen minutes, and make no mistake – it is hard work! Sit, stand, walk about from room to room, sing to yourself, do anything to while away the time, but go on beating until the mixture clings stiffly to the fork. Now fold in three tablespoonfuls of castor sugar.

Spread the meringue over the cooled plums in the *soufflé* dish. See that it comes right to the edge of the dish and leaves no space uncovered. Wipe away any bits from the rim or sides. Put the dish in the oven and cook at the lowest possible heat for from three to three and a half hours. Don't be dismayed if at the end of three hours you open the oven door and find the meringue looking exactly as it did when you first put it in. Eventually it will turn a very pale golden colour, and the top will have a slightly blistered appearance. It should feel crisp when touched.

Patience, a strong wrist and an oven that will maintain a constant, very low heat are all that is needed to make a success of this recipe. You may prove by experiment that it is equally good when other fruits – e.g., apples, cherries, apricots or gooseberries are used instead of plums.

SHOPPING LIST

						s.	d.
Poulterer.							
1 guinea-fowl, trussed, with larding bacon					...	3	0
Dairy.							
¼ lb. butter	...	...	...	...	...	0	3
Cream ...	...	...	...	...	...	0	4
3 eggs ...	...	...	...	...	...	0	4½
Delicatessen Shop.							
9 olives ...	...	...	...	...	...	0	3
Greengrocer.							
2 lbs. peas	...	...	...	...	...	0	4
1 lb. potatoes	...	...	...	...	...	0	1½
1½ lbs. purple plums (small) ...		...	...	...	...	0	3
From Stock.							
6 ozs. sugar	...	...	...	...	...	0	1
						5	0

TIME-TABLE

N.B. – If you are dining at a different time, calculate from the time-table at what hour you will have to start your preparations and then alter the hands of the kitchen clock to conform with the time-table. You will find it easier than making individual calculations over every item.

The sweet for this dinner must be made beforehand, preferably on the same day, but, if this is impossible, on the previous evening. The plums will take five minutes to prepare, ten to cook, and at least thirty to cool. The meringue will take twenty minutes. Do not allow yourself less than an hour before putting the dish in the oven – i.e., if you make it between six and seven in the evening, it should be finished by ten to ten-thirty, or supposing you make it by one o'clock, it should be cooked by tea-time, and be pleasantly cold in time for dinner.

Leave yourself twenty-five minutes for the stuffing. You may not take so much time, but it will give you confidence to have it in hand.

6	0	Shell peas.
6	15	Peel and cut up potatoes.
6	30	Start making stuffing.
6	40	*Light oven.* Continue stuffing.
6	55	Put stuffed guinea-fowl in fast oven – lid of roaster *off*.
		Baste during next fifteen minutes.
7	10	*Lower heat slightly*, put lid on roaster.
7	15	Start boiling potatoes.

LAY THE TABLE

7	25	*Start boiling salted water for peas.*
		If cream is not sour, add vinegar.

PUT PLATES AND DISHES TO WARM

7	30	*Drain and dry potatoes.*
		Heat milk. Add milk to potatoes, mash together.

7 35 *Start boiling peas.*
Beat yolks of two eggs.
Add beaten yolks, pepper and salt to potatoes.

7 40 *Lower oven heat considerably.*
Put potatoes in oven.

7 50 *Drain peas,* remove mint, put peas in dish.
Turn oven heat down as low as possible.

7 53 *Remove guinea-fowl from roaster,* cut string, remove
larding bacon and skewer, put on dish in oven.
Start simmering gravy in roaster.
Add sour cream and stir well.
Season.

8 0 Pour sauce into gravy boat, arrange peas on dish
and serve.

If people have not arrived by 7.55, or if you know that
they will be late, leave the guinea-fowl in the closed roaster
and turn down the oven as low as possible. It is unwise to
start on your sauce until the guests have actually arrived –
only do not forget that the guinea-fowl must only be kept
warm, not cooked, after an hour, and the heat of the oven
must be reduced just as far as it will go. Neither peas nor
potatoes will come to harm where they are.

SPINACH SOUP

HAM AND STEAK ROLL (COLD)

MAYONNAISE OF BROAD BEANS

SOUFFLE OF POTATOES

ROTHE GRUTZE

(Raspberry and Red Currant Mould)

This is a dinner for a very hot evening in July. Broad beans, raspberries and red currants should all be in season. Spinach, which will be coarser now than in spring and early summer, is used in a *purée* for the soup, which you can serve hot or cold. The various dishes in this menu take some time to cook, but everything except the potatoes can be prepared beforehand. In this way the hostess may remain cool and unworried up to the last moment.

RECIPE 1.

Spinach Soup. (Cost: about 5d.)

1 lb. spinach	Pepper, salt
1 oz. flour	Water
1 oz. butter	

Buy a pound of spinach. Pluck the leaves from the stems and wash them thoroughly in several waters. Shake the leaves dry in a cloth.

Boil a pint of water with a dessertspoonful of salt. When it boils, throw in the spinach and cook it for three or four minutes with the lid of the saucepan off. Drain the spinach in a colander, collecting the water in which it was boiled in a bowl placed under the colander. Set the water aside. Put the spinach under the cold tap, run water through it and, as soon as it is cool enough, squeeze it thoroughly with your hands. It will seem an alarmingly small quantity, but do not let this worry you. Place a hair sieve over a large basin and rub the spinach through the sieve with a wooden spoon.

(N.B. – Rubbing anything through a sieve is hard work and takes some time. Keep on mashing the stuff to and fro, crushing and squashing it with the back of the spoon until nothing but stringy or hard portions, or, in the case of fruit, pips, seeds, skin or stones is left. Look at the under side of the sieve from time to time; a rich pulp will be clinging there and can be scraped off into the basin with a clean spoon – the one used for rubbing may have just the bits you want to avoid clinging to it. Rub everything as much as possible across the centre of the sieve, or it may miss the basin if it is not a very large one.)

Heat an ounce of butter in a saucepan and when it is melted and very hot add a tablespoonful of flour. Work the flour into the butter with a wooden spoon, then take the saucepan to the edge of the stove and add, little by little and stirring hard all the time, a breakfastcupful of the water in which the spinach was boiled. When the mixture is really smooth, return the saucepan to the flame and stir until the sauce boils gently all over. Let it boil for a few minutes, then add the sieved spinach and stir it well into the rest. Now add another breakfastcupful and a half of hot water, or stock (not more of the water in which the spinach boiled). Taste and season. Simmer and stir for a minute or so longer, then stop stirring and just simmer with the lid of the saucepan off for thirty minutes longer or until the soup is needed – but take care not to boil away too much of the soup. If left to get cold, it can be gently reheated over a low flame or, on the other hand, you may serve it cold.

Serve in small marmite pots, one for each person.

Recipe 2.
Ham and Steak Roll. (Cost: about 1/7½.)

½ lb. English beef steak	½ teaspoonful mixed dried
6 oz. cooked ham (lean)	herbs.
1 egg	¼ teaspoonful mace
2 ozs. fresh breadcrumbs	Pepper, salt
2 tablespoonfuls brown crumbs	

Buy half a pound of English beef steak, as lean as you can get it, and six ounces of cooked ham, also as lean as possible. Wipe the meat and cut off any skin or fat, and cut off most of the fat from the ham.

Mince the beef and ham on to a large plate or into a bowl. If the mincer gets too wet, put a dry crust through it. This will dry the mincer and blend with the meat.

(N.B. – Mincing raw meat is not a very pleasant job, but it is worth doing it yourself rather than buying meat already minced from the butcher, as this is apt to be rather tough and flavourless. Be sure, immediately you have finished with it, to take the mincer to pieces and plunge every part of it into hot – if possible boiling – water. Every crack and cranny is apt to retain particles of raw meat and fat unless these are immediately loosened by the hot water.)

Crumble about half a teacupful of fresh crumbs with your fingers or by rubbing the bread through a colander. If the bread is too new to crumble, put some slices in a slow oven and leave them until they are dry enough to crumble.

Beat an egg, yolk and white together, for a minute. Grease the inside of a china jam-pot thoroughly.

Now mix the minced beef and ham with the breadcrumbs in a basin. Add half a teaspoonful of dried herbs and a quarter of a teaspoonful of mace. Mix well and add the beaten egg. Season with a teaspoonful of salt and a quarter of a teaspoonful of pepper. Stir the whole mixture round thoroughly, then ram it into the greased jam-pot. Tie some greased paper tightly round the top of the jam-pot and prick it with a fork in one or two places. Leave loops of string, if possible, at either side of the jam-pot, in order to lift it when it is hot. Place the jam-pot in the top half of a steamer over BOILING water and steam it for three hours. Take care to replenish the water in the bottom half of the steamer with fresh BOILING water when the water there gets low. Do not worry if some liquid runs out of the holes in the greased paper as the roll is cooking. This is quite likely to happen and the roll will survive.

After three hours let the jam-pot cool slightly, and meanwhile put two tablespoonfuls of browned crumbs (which you can buy in economical small packets from the grocer) on to a plate. Slide the roll out of the jam-pot on to this plate and roll it until it is coated with crumbs. Put in a cool place.

Serve cold and decorate, if you like, with a few small, absolutely fresh and well-washed sprigs of mint, thyme or parsley, or with some flowers – golden marigold heads in a ring, or nasturtiums mixed with their leaves.

RECIPE 3.
Mayonnaise of Broad Beans. (Cost: about 9d.)

2 lbs. broad beans	2 or 3 spring onions
1 egg	A little parsley
About 1 gill salad oil	Pepper, salt
1 tablespoonful tarragon vinegar	

Quite old broad beans may be used for this dish. Buy two pounds, shell them and wash them and put them into plenty of boiling, salted water. Boil them rather quickly with the lid of the saucepan off for about twenty minutes, or until tender – fish one out with a fork, cool it and try.

When the beans are cooked, turn them out into the colander and let the cold tap run through them until they are cool. Drain them, slip them gently out of their skins with your fingers, throw the skins away and put the beans aside in a basin in a cool place until you want them. Mix them just before serving with the following flavoured Mayonnaise sauce.

Mayonnaise sauce. Crack an egg against the edge of a bowl and break it in two, letting the white drip down into the bowl while you turn the yolk from one half of the shell to the other until it is perfectly free of white. Set the white aside. Put the yolk in a bowl and beat it with a fork for a few seconds. Now add a few drops of salad oil and beat them into the egg. Repeat this addition of oil once or twice, then take your courage in both hands and add oil freely. Go on beating and adding liberal doses of oil until the sauce is quite stiff. Taste the sauce – if it tastes 'floury', you have added enough oil; if it tastes 'eggy', you must go on adding oil. The sauce should look very pale and creamy.

Now add a few drops of water and a teaspoonful of tarragon vinegar to the sauce. Stir. The sauce will instantly thin out a little. Go on adding vinegar and stirring it into the sauce until the taste satisfies you. Then add pepper and salt to your taste and finally a very few spring onions, finely chopped, and a little chopped parsley.

Set the sauce aside in a cool place until it is wanted. Mix it with the broad beans just before serving. DROP THE BROAD BEANS INTO THE BOWL CONTAINING THE SAUCE and turn them about very gently with a wooden spoon and fork, or two wooden spoons, until they are thoroughly coated with mayonnaise.

(N.B. – This recipe is flat heresy, but it works. Pay no attention to the 'drop by drop to the bitter end' theory advanced by all high-class cooks. It does not take six eggs and sixty minutes to make a good mayonnaise sauce – you can make one in six minutes if you like. Beat steadily and take care not to go too fast in the first minute or two, that is all.)

RECIPE 4.
Soufflé of Potatoes. (Cost: about 4d.)

1 lb. potatoes	1 yolk and 2 whites of egg
2 tablespoonfuls milk	Pepper, salt
½ oz. butter	

Peel a pound of potatoes and cut them into slices about half an inch thick. Put these into enough boiling, salted water to cover them and boil them rather quickly with the lid of the saucepan almost closed until they are cooked through. This will take about ten to fifteen minutes – test them with a knitting-needle and see when they are done. Drain them, dry the saucepan, return the potatoes to the saucepan and set it by the edge of the stove so that the potatoes may dry.

You have one white of egg left over from the mayonnaise. Separate the white of another egg from the yolk in the same way. Beat the yolk with a fork for a minute. Beat the whites with another fork until they are fairly stiff (about five minutes). Warm two tablespoonfuls of milk in a saucepan.

Now add the warm milk, together with about half an ounce of butter to the potatoes and mash them thoroughly with a fork until there is not a trace of a lump left. The whole secret of a good potato *purée* lies in a really thorough mashing. As soon as your *purée* is smooth, add the beaten yolk and mix it well in. Season to taste. Give the whites of egg a good final beating for a minute and mix them smoothly into the potato.

Grease a *soufflé* dish, pile in the potato and cook it, uncovered, for from fifteen to twenty minutes in a rather quick oven. The potato should puff up and brown just a little at the top.

Serve in the dish it was cooked in. This is a *soufflé* that neither rises high nor falls fast and it may in consequence be kept waiting without any humiliating results.

RECIPE 5.
Rothe Grütze. (Cost: about 1/10.)

1 lb. red currants	1 tablespoonful cornflour
½ lb. raspberries	Water (about 1 gill)
¼ lb. castor sugar	

Wash and pick the stalks from one pound of red

currants and half a pound of raspberries. Then squeeze the fruit through a piece of muslin into a bowl. Press with your fingers until all the juice has run through, but don't go on until you begin to force seeds or skin through the muslin as this is just what you want to avoid. Put the juice in a saucepan, add a teacupful of water and a quarter of a pound of castor sugar and bring slowly to the boil, stirring with a wooden spoon.

Sieve a tablespoonful of cornflour and mix it with a very little water in a saucer until it makes a smooth, thin paste, like cream. Add this to the fruit juice (which must have reached boiling-point), stirring all the time. The juice will go off the boil when you add the cornflour; bring it gently to the boil again and simmer it for eight or nine minutes, still stirring until you feel the liquid thickening and turning sticky under your spoon.

Pour into a wet mould and leave in a cool place to set. This will not take very long – half to three-quarters of an hour. Turn out when wanted into a glass dish. If the fruit is inclined to stick to the mould, press it down round the edges or slip a pastry-knife round between the fruit and the mould. Just before serving, pour sixpennyworth of unwhipped, unsweetened cream round, but not over, the fruit. The beautiful, deep colour should be left unspoiled.

(N.B. – You can use tinned fruit, or different fresh fruits, to make a similar sweet. But tinned fruits have

not the same delicious fresh taste, and raspberries
and red currants are an ideal mixture).

SHOPPING LIST

Butcher.

					s.	d.
½ lb. beef steak (English)	...	...	...		0	9

Dairy.

Cream	...	...	...	...	...	...	0	6
3 eggs	...	...	...	...	...	...	0	4½

Greengrocer.

1 lb. spinach	...	...	...	...	...	0	4
2 lbs. broad beans	...	...	...	...	0	5
1 lb. potatoes	...	...	...	...	...	0	1½
1 lb. red currants	...	...	...	...	0	10
½ lb. raspberries	...	...	...	...	0	5

Grocer.

6 ozs. cooked ham (lean)	...	...	...	0	9

From Stock.

1½ ozs. butter for soup and potatoes ...	...	0	1½
Oil, for mayonnaise ...	...	...	...	0	2
Vinegar, for mayonnaise	...	...	...	0	0½
¼ lb. castor sugar	...	...	...	...	0	1
Parsley, milk ...	...	...	...	...	0	0½
Flour, bread crumbs, herbs, mace, spring onions, cornflour ...	...	...	...	...	0	0½

	5 0

SEVEN DINNERS FOR SUMMER

TIME-TABLE

Dinner at Eight O'Clock

N.B. – If you are dining at a different time, calculate from the time-table the hour at which you will have to start your preparations and then alter the hands of the kitchen clock to conform with the time-table. You will find it easier than making individual calculations over every item.

The ham and steak roll for this meal must be made beforehand so as to get perfectly cold. Even if the weather is very hot, the cooked roll will keep excellently overnight. The sweet should also be made beforehand. Cook both on the previous evening or, if you have time, on the morning of the day on which they are to be eaten.

The roll will take three hours to cook and must be looked at from time to time to see that the water is always boiling below it. The sweet will not take more than three-quarters of an hour. You might, therefore, just as well prepare the soup, beans and mayonnaise at the same time. The soup will take about forty minutes to prepare, thirty minutes to simmer – one hour, ten minutes in all. The beans should be shelled, cooked and their jackets taken off in forty to fifty minutes. The mayonnaise can be made in about ten minutes and SHOULD NOT HAVE THE ONIONS AND PARSLEY ADDED UNTIL JUST BEFORE DINNER.

Roll	... ...	4 hours ($\frac{1}{2}$ to prepare, $3\frac{1}{2}$ to cook)
Sweet	... ...	45 minutes
Soup	... ...	1 hour 10 minutes
Beans	... ...	50 minutes
Mayonnaise	...	15 minutes

Therefore, as you can see, the cooking of sweet, soup, beans and mayonnaise only takes 3 hours altogether and you will have plenty of time to complete it and wash up while the roll is being cooked.

Leave the soup in the saucepan ready for reheating, if you want to have it hot. Put the beans and mayonnaise in separate bowls in the coolest place you can find. Leave the sweet in the mould.

THERE ARE NO PLATES OR DISHES TO BE WARMED FOR THIS DINNER UNLESS YOU ARE HAVING THE SOUP HOT

7 0   *Start boiling salted water for potatoes.*
       Peel and slice potatoes.
7 10 *Start boiling potatoes.*

LAY THE TABLE

7 20 If soup is to be served hot, start reheating it gently and put marmite pots or bowls to warm over plate-rack, covered with cloth.

7 25 (about – test) *Drain potatoes.* Dry saucepan. *Light oven.*

7 27 *Put potatoes back in saucepan near flame to dry.*
       Separate egg, beat yolk and two whites.
       Warm milk.

7 35 (*about*) Mash potatoes with butter and milk. Add yolk, stir well.
       Season, add whites.
       Put all in greased fireproof dish.

7 40 *Start cooking potato soufflé in oven.*
       Turn out sweet, pour cream round.
       Prepare parsley and onion, add to mayonnaise. Put beans in bowl with mayonnaise, coat gently, turn out into dish.

If guests are late, nothing will suffer. Most of the food is cold, the soup (if you are having it hot) can be kept simmering over a low flame. Cover the potatoes and leave them in the oven with the flame turned down as low as possible.

BAKED HAM

BROAD BEANS

NEW POTATOES

STRAWBERRY SHORTCAKE

This is a meal for the middle of summer, when broad beans and strawberries are at their best and cheapest. Earlier in the year it would be impossible to have the whole meal for 5/-.

RECIPE 1.

Baked Ham. (Cost: about 2/8.)

1½ lbs. gammon rasher	1 tablespoonful mustard (dry)
1 tablespoonful flour	1 tablespoonful brown sugar
1 teacupful milk	

Buy one and a half pounds of gammon rasher, about three-quarters of an inch thick. If it is a large piece of bacon, one slice will probably be enough. If not, get two slices. Do not buy one thicker slice. The meat is very close, and the whole dish rather rich, so that a piece two or three inches square is enough for most people.

Soak the gammon all day or overnight in plenty of cold water, changing it once or twice. Just before

133

you cook the bacon, put it in a saucepan with enough cold water to cover it, bring it slowly to the boil and simmer for a minute or two.

These preliminaries are not absolutely necessary, but the bacon is likely to be salt and tough if they are omitted.

Now take one tablespoonful of flour, one of dry mustard and one of brown sugar. Mix them well together. If you do not do this thoroughly, gusts of mustard will choke the eaters and the flour will turn pasty in cooking.

Rub this mixture boldly into the bacon on both sides with the back of a spoon until it is well coated. Put the ham in a flat fireproof dish and cover it with the remains of the flour, mustard and sugar mixture.

Now pour in at the side enough milk to come to the same level as the ham, *but not to cover it*, except here and there, perhaps, in a valley. A teacupful of milk will be quite enough. Pour it in slowly so as not to flood the dish.

Bake, uncovered, in a moderate oven for thirty to forty minutes. When the dish is cooked the liquid milk should have entirely disappeared and the ham be lightly masked and surrounded with a creamy, yellowish mixture having about the appearance and consistency of melted cheese.

RECIPE 2.
Broad Beans. (Cost: about 8½d.)

4 lbs. broad beans	Pepper, salt
¼ oz. butter	
A squeeze of lemon juice	

You will need three or four pounds of young broad beans for four people. Take them out of their shells and put them into a saucepan of boiling salted water without a lid. Boil them for fifteen minutes fairly rapidly, and test them carefully at the end of that time – or even sooner, if they look very young – by picking one or two out and eating them. It is very important indeed not to cook them a moment too long or the taste will be gone.

When they are ready, turn them out into a colander and drain them well. If the beans are very young and fresh the skins will be tender enough to eat. Otherwise it is as well to take the skins off *when the beans are cooked*. They will come off at a flick of the fingers then, and the skins form some protection to the beans while they are cooking.

Put them in a hot vegetable dish with a generous piece of butter. Put on the lid and toss them around for a moment or two to distribute the butter. Add a squeeze of lemon juice. This is especially desirable in this menu, as the ham is so rich in flavour. A slight sharpness in the vegetable is a welcome contrast. Season with pepper and a little salt.

RECIPE 3.
New potatoes.

Put a pound or so of new potatoes into boiling salted water with a sprig of mint and boil for twenty minutes with the lid half on. Test carefully with a metal skewer or a steel knitting-needle to see whether they are done. Drain them in a colander and place them in a hot vegetable dish. Spread them with a little butter, or if you have a butter dish with some remains in it, or a piece of paper in which the butter has been wrapped, invert one of them over the potatoes. This is a good economy, for it uses up the unusable and gives just the right amount of butter to the potatoes. Sprinkle the potatoes with a little finely-chopped parsley.

RECIPE 4.
Strawberry Shortcake. (Cost: about 1/6.)

6 ozs. flour	4 teaspoonfuls baking powder
1 saltspoonful salt	A little milk
2 ozs. sugar	1½ lbs. strawberries
A little icing sugar	

This is an American recipe to which cream can be added if you like, although the dish is then so rich that it is apt to make even the best trenchermen feel a little bloated. The original American recipes contain no egg, although this is almost always included in versions of this sweet given in English cookery books. The latter may be very good sweets, but they are not strawberry shortcake.

Buy a pound and a half of strawberries. They need not be the best, as they are to be crushed. Wash and stalk the strawberries. Select the twelve best specimens for decoration and crush the rest with two or three tablespoonfuls of sugar. There is no need to go through the arduous business of a sieve with such a tender fruit, especially as it does not need to be crushed to a *purée*, but rather to the resemblance of jam. Leave it aside in a cool place, and make the shortcake.

The Shortcake.

Sift together one and a half cups of flour (six ounces) and four – yes, *four* – teaspoonfuls of baking powder, and a saltspoonful of salt. Cut in with a knife a bare two ounces of butter. Cut this up into the smallest pieces you can amongst the flour, but do not touch it with your hands. Now add a tablespoonful of cold milk and with your hands form the paste into a dough. If you need a little more milk before the paste becomes cohesive, add another tablespoonful – no more. Work as quickly as you can, and handle the dough as little as possible. It should be very stiff and leave the sides of the basin clean.

Flour a rolling-pin and turn the dough on to a floured board. Roll the dough (in one direction only) to fit the pan in which it is to be baked. This should preferably be a baking tin about 8 inches by 4 inches and about 1 inch deep, but a circular one will do, provided it is not too large for the dough.

Remember all this must be done quickly.

Bake the shortcake in a quick oven for twenty minutes. It will rise considerably.

When it is done (it should be golden in colour) take it out of the oven and let it cool *in the pan* for a few minutes. Then turn it out and cut it in two lengthwise through the middle with a sharp knife, so that it forms two layers. Spread the lower half with a thick layer of the crushed strawberries and some of the juice – not too much, or the cake will become soggy. Cover with the top half, and decorate with the twelve whole strawberries and a little powdered icing sugar.

Whipped cream may be interposed between the strawberries and the top layer, if you have decided to use it and do not mind the extra expense. Strawberry shortcake is best eaten while the shortcake part of it is still warm, like a fresh cake. But it can be eaten cold with success, in which case it must be left to cool on a cake-rack or the top of a sieve. In each case, the strawberries and the cream, if you are using any, must be very cold.

This mixture (the shortcake) can well be eaten with other fruits or with jam.

SHOPPING LIST

				s.	d.
Greengrocer.					
4 lbs. broad beans	... ...	...	...		8
1 lb. new potatoes	... ...	...	...		1½
1½ lbs. strawberries (not the best)		...	...	1	3
Grocer.					
1½ lbs. gammon ...	... ...	...	...	2	6
From Stock.					
7 ozs. flour ...	... ...	...	...		1
1 tablespoonful mustard, 1 tablespoonful brown sugar, 4 teaspoonfuls baking powder, 3 ozs. castor sugar	... ...	...	...		1
1 gill milk ...	... ...	...	...		¾
2 ozs. butter	... ...	...	...		2
Parsley, mint	... ...	...	...	0	1
				5	0¼

TIME-TABLE

DINNER AT EIGHT O'CLOCK

N.B. – If you are dining at a different time, calculate from the time-table at what hour you will have to start your preparations and then alter the hands of the kitchen clock to conform with the time-table. You will find it easier than making individual calculations over every item.

———

OVERNIGHT. Soak ham.

6 15   LAY THE TABLE

6 30   *Light oven for shortcake.*
        Make shortcake.

6 40   *Put shortcake in oven.* While it is baking prepare the fruit.

6 50   Scrape potatoes.
       Shell beans.

7 0   *Take shortcake out of oven* and leave it to cool.
       Turn out oven.
       Take ham out of soak and start to bring to boil.

7 05   Cut shortcake in two and fill with fruit.
       Set aside, ready for the table.

7 12   Take ham out of water and prepare it for baking.
       Light oven for ham.

7 20   *Put ham in oven.*

PUT PLATES AND DISHES TO WARM

7 30   *Put salted water on to boil for beans and potatoes.*
       Chop parsley for potatoes.

7 40   *Put beans and potatoes on to boil.*

7 50   Test beans.

7 55   *Take out beans, if not already done.*
       Drain and toss in butter. Season.

8 0   *Take out potatoes,* drain and put in hot vegetable dish with butter and parsley.
       Serve ham in the dish in which it was cooked.

If people are late, keep the ham in its dish, but cover it. Keep beans and potatoes in hot vegetable dishes on top of the oven where they will remain hot for some time. Keep the oven at a very low heat.

VEAL CHOPS

NEW POTATOES COOKED IN BUTTER (RISSOLE)

CARROTS A LA VICHY

GLOBE ARTICHOKES

CREAM TARTS

You will only be able to afford globe artichokes about once a year in a 5/– menu, as they are generally sold for from fourpence to eightpence each. Sometimes, however, at the very height of summer, they cost only threepence each. Then is the time to seize these delicacies and eat them while you may.

RECIPE I.

Veal Chops. (Cost: about 2/2.)

> 4 veal chops   Juice of half a lemon
> 3 ozs. lard or bacon fat Pepper, salt

Ask your butcher to cut you four good veal chops from the loin. Wipe them.

Heat about three ounces of fat – lard or bacon fat is best – until a faint smoke rises from the frying-pan. Then put in the cutlets and fry them for two minutes on each side. After this, very slightly lower the heat (it must continue HOT however, or the chops will become greasy) and continue to cook for about fifteen minutes. You must give the cutlets all your attention and turn them frequently with two spoons. Underdone veal is really distasteful and the chops would be better over- rather than under-cooked.

(We do not suggest first coating the chops in egg and breadcrumbs, as this would make them too heavy. However, if you have a passion for food fried in this way, you should dip the chops first in slightly beaten egg and then in browned crumbs, then fry them as described above. A lighter way would be to dip the chops in flour seasoned with a little pepper and salt.)

Lift out the chops on a fish-slice and drain them on a piece of soft paper on an enamel plate. Cover the plate and keep it hot in the oven with the heat very low.

Serve the chops on a hot dish with gravy poured over them.

Gravy for Veal.

Pour nearly all the fat away from the frying-pan and give what is left a good stir round, bringing into it everything that is left sticking to the sides or bottom of the pan. Add to this about a teacupful of stock, if you have any, or, if you have not, a teacupful of the water in which the potatoes have boiled. Add a teaspoonful of lemon juice. Taste and add pepper and salt if necessary. Let the gravy simmer for a few minutes.

When you dish up the veal, strain the gravy over the chops and scatter over the top a little finely-chopped parsley. There should not be a lake of gravy, but just enough to moisten the cutlets thoroughly.

RECIPE 2.

New Potatoes Cooked in Butter. (*Rissolé.*) (Cost: about 3½d.)

1 lb. small new potatoes	Sprig of mint
2 or 3 ozs. butter	Salt

Buy some small new potatoes, which should now be very cheap. Scrape these and make them as much of one size as possible – they should look like little balls.

Put them in a saucepan of boiling salted water with a sprig of mint and boil, with the lid half on, for from ten to fifteen minutes – until, in fact, they are nearly, but not quite, soft. (Test with a knitting-needle.) Drain the potatoes very thoroughly and dry them for a minute in the dry, empty saucepan by the flame. KEEP THE POTATO WATER TO MAKE GRAVY.

Now melt two or three ounces of butter in a clean, dry saucepan. The exact amount of butter will depend on the size of the saucepan – it should be sufficient to cover the potatoes when it starts to froth. Put the well-dried and nearly cooked potatoes in the butter and shake them about on a fairly hot flame for from five to ten minutes, until they are golden all over. They should still be perfectly soft outside. Take them out with a strainer spoon and put them on some soft paper in a hot vegetable dish;

the paper will absorb any superfluous fat which may be clinging to them. Just before serving the potatoes, slip away the paper and sprinkle them with fine, dry salt.

RECIPE 3.
Carrots *à la Vichy*. (Cost: about 5d.)

1 lb. young carrots	1 dessertspoonful sugar
1 oz. butter	1 teaspoonful salt

Buy a pound of young carrots, which must not be old enough to have any appreciable core. Scrape them lightly and cut them into rounds about the thickness of a florin.

Put the rings in a saucepan with enough water to cover them, an ounce of butter, a dessertspoonful of sugar and a teaspoonful of salt. Bring to the boil and boil quickly, with the lid off, for about thirty minutes, by which time (or even earlier) the water will have disappeared and the carrots will be beginning to brown in the butter which has mysteriously survived the boiling. Let the carrots brown for a minute, then turn them out into a hot dish, pour anything left in the saucepan over them and sprinkle them with a little finely-chopped parsley.

RECIPE 4.
Globe Artichokes. (Cost: about 1/3.)

4 globe artichokes	Juice of half a lemon
4 ozs. butter	Salt, pepper

These artichokes are thistle-like in form and only

the leaves and the base are edible. Cut off the stems and any discoloured outside leaves. Wash, leaving head downwards in a bowl of salted water for half an hour or longer. Then rinse the artichokes well under the tap and put them head downwards in a saucepan of boiling salted water with a few drops of lemon juice. Boil them rapidly, with the lid off, for ten minutes, then reduce heat and simmer them for thirty minutes, or until the leaves can be easily detached. Turn them out of the saucepan and drain thoroughly.

Just before serving the artichokes, melt a quarter of a pound of butter with some pepper and salt in a very clean saucepan and warm four egg-cups or tiny *soufflé* dishes. Fill each egg-cup or dish with melted butter, to which you must add a very little strained lemon juice. Serve the artichokes on separate plates with an egg-cup of butter for each person. (Melted butter for artichokes is usually served from a sauce-boat, but this causes the butter to run about the plate and does not make it possible – as the egg-cup method does – for each person to dip just the part of the leaf that is necessary into the butter without soaking all the rest in grease.)

The melting of the butter should be done between courses, as the artichokes are served in a course to themselves – or you could fill your egg-cups before-hand and leave them in the bottom of a very, very gentle oven.

145

RECIPE 5.

Cream Tarts. (Cost: about 10½d.)

¼ lb. flour	3 tablespoonfuls jam
4 ozs. lard	6d. worth cream
¼ teaspoonful baking powder	Pinch of salt

Make some short pastry thus:

Sift half a pound of flour, together with a quarter of a teaspoonful of baking powder and a pinch of salt, into a basin through a sieve or strainer. Put four ounces of lard into the flour and cut it up into small pieces. Now rub the fat into the flour lightly and quickly with your finger-tips, lifting the flour as you do so – and do all this in a COOL part of the kitchen. When all the lard is rubbed into the flour (and there must not be the smallest lump of fat left), the mixture should look like fine breadcrumbs. Gather it all up and make a little hole in the middle; pour a dessertspoonful of cold water into this hole and mix it well in with a pastry-knife. Then add another dessertspoonful and mix in again quickly. If the mixture is still very dry, cautiously add another dessertspoonful. You should now have a stiff paste in the basin; press this together and knead it with the knuckles of your hands until it forms a firm ball of dough that leaves the sides of the basin quite clean.

Turn this ball of dough out on to a floured board and knead again for a minute, coaxing all cracks from the dough by gentle pressure.

Flour your rolling-pin and roll out the pastry. Roll lightly and quickly in one direction – away from

146

you – lifting the pastry from time to time and turning it to your left, so that a fresh piece is in front of
you. Be careful to roll evenly so that the middle and
edges are all of the same thickness.

With a pastry-cutter cut circles from the dough to
fit your patty-pans. (This amount of pastry should
fill twelve or fourteen small pans.) Ease the circles
gently into the tins, mark the edges with the pastry-
knife, and prick the bottom of each tart with a fork.

Put about a teaspoonful of whatever kind of jam you
prefer into each tart (being careful to see that none is
spilt on the tin and that no tart is overful – a very little
jam in each is enough). Bake in a quick oven until the
pastry is pale golden brown round the edges – about
twenty minutes. When the tarts are cooked let them
cool in the patty-pans, then slip them out on to a plate
with a pastry-knife. Just before serving, whip up sixpennyworth of cream stiffly and put a cap of cream
on each tart.

SHOPPING LIST

						s.	d.
Butcher.							
4 veal chops	...	...	...	...	...	2	0
Dairy.							
½ lb. butter	...	...	...	...	...	0	6
Cream	...	...	...	...	...	0	6
Greengrocer.							
1 lemon	...	...	...	...	...	0	1
1 lb. new potatoes (small)		...	...	...	0	1½
1 lb. young carrots	...	...	...	...	0	4
4 globe artichokes	...	...	...	...	1	0
From Stock.							
7 ozs. lard	...	...	...	...	...	0	3½
½ lb. flour	...	...	...	...	...	0	1½
Jam ...	...	...	...	...	...	0	1
						5	0½

Parsley, mint, sugar, baking powder, negligible.

TIME-TABLE

Dinner at Eight O'Clock

N.B. – If you are dining at a different hour, calculate from the time-table at what time you will have to start your preparations and then alter the hands of the kitchen clock to conform with the time-table. You will find this easier than making individual calculations over every item.

This is not a particularly easy meal to prepare, as everything but the sweet is being cooked at the same time on the top of the stove. Therefore do not cook it until you have some experience, particularly if your guests weigh on your mind. It is not a good meal to keep waiting and should be chosen for punctual people.

Beforehand. Put artichokes to soak in salted water.

5 45   *Light oven.*
         Make tarts.
6 0   *Put tarts in oven.*

WASH UP

LAY THE TABLE

    Wash, dry and chop a little parsley.
6 20 *Take tarts from oven* and leave to cool.
        Scrape potatoes.
        Scrape carrots and cut into rings.
6 30 Assemble frying-pan, saucepans for vegetables, lard, butter, mint, salt, pepper, sugar. Squeeze and strain lemon juice. Have soft paper handy for draining fried food.
        PUT PLATES AND DISHES TO WARM IN RACK
6 50 *Start boiling salted water for artichokes.*
7 0   *Start boiling artichokes rapidly.*
        Start boiling salted water for potatoes.
7 10 *Turn down artichokes to simmer.*
        Start boiling potatoes.
7 20 *Drain potatoes, leave to dry.* KEEP WATER FOR GRAVY.
        Put carrots in saucepan with water, butter, sugar, salt, start cooking.
7 30 Whip cream for tarts, pile on top and leave tarts ready for table.
7 38 *Start heating lard for chops.*
        Light oven.

149

7 40   *Melt butter for potatoes,* and artichokes.

      Start frying chops.

      Put melted butter for artichokes in bottom of oven, or under grill.

7 42   *Start cooking potatoes in butter.*

      Now go on shaking the potatoes, keeping an eye on the carrots and occasionally turning the veal until :

7 50   *Take out potatoes* and put on soft paper on enamel plate. Put plate in bottom of oven, covered.

      Carrots will now be sizzling in butter, so turn them out into a hot dish, pour butter over, if any left, and sprinkle with chopped parsley.

7 55   *Stop frying chops,* put on soft paper on plate. Put plate in oven and cover.

      Make gravy.

      Drain artichokes, place in hot dish.

      (If you prefer to melt the butter for the artichokes between courses, do so. If not, remember to leave the oven just alight to keep the melted butter warm.)

This is NOT a good meal to keep back. However, if people are late, you must leave the veal and potatoes, both covered, in the oven, with the heat very low. Put the hot vegetable dish containing the carrots in the oven. Leave the drained artichokes in the (dried) saucepan in which you boiled them and cover it with a clean dry cloth to prevent them getting damp and cold. Strain the gravy into a boat or jug and stand this in a pan of gently-boiling water.

GRILLED LAMB CUTLETS
MINT SAUCE (Optional)
DEVONSHIRE FRIED POTATOES
RUNNER BEANS

MILKY RICE PUDDING WITH CHERRIES

RECIPE 1.
Grilled Lamb Cutlets. (Cost: about 2/6½.)

10 lamb cutlets   A few springs of parsley
A little olive oil

Buy ten lamb cutlets from the neck. New Zealand lamb would do very well, in which case the cutlets would be cheaper and you could afford to include mint sauce in the dinner. This is quite a cheap meal, however, so, unless you particularly crave for mint sauce, you might as well buy English or Scotch meat. Get the butcher to trim the cutlets; if, instead of buying them separately, you buy a piece of best end of neck and tell the butcher to prepare the cutlets for grilling, and to send you the trimmings, you will have some bones from which you can make a small quantity of stock by putting them (well washed) into a saucepan with cold water to cover, pepper, salt, an onion and a carrot peeled and cut in quarters and a bouquet of herbs or a pinch of dried herbs tied up in muslin; bring the water very, very slowly to the boil and simmer it gently for an hour or so.

To grill your cutlets, light the grill and make the frets of the grill red hot and the grid itself very hot indeed. Meanwhile brush the cutlets over with a little good olive oil on both sides, using a pastry-brush. Range the cutlets in rows on the hot grid, put it under the grill and cook the cutlets for a minute on each side at very fierce heat. Then lower the heat a little and continue to cook the cutlets for four or five minutes, turning them once during that time.

Pile them up on a very hot dish and put a few sprigs of well-washed and dried parsley around them. Serve the Devonshire fried potatoes on the same dish – cutlets always have a rather forlorn air by themselves.

RECIPE 2.
Mint Sauce (optional). (Cost: about 2d.)

1 bunch of mint	3 tablespoonfuls vinegar
1 dessertspoonful white sugar	

Wash a bunch of mint, dry it and pick the leaves from the stalks. Put these in a heap on a chopping-board, sprinkle them with white sugar and chop. As you chop, add more white sugar from time to time, until you have used at least a dessertspoonful. Chop the mint very finely, then put it in a little jug and add only enough tarragon vinegar to make a very thick sauce. Mint and sugar should be the basis of the sauce, not vinegar.

RECIPE 3.
Devonshire Fried Potatoes. (Cost: about 4d.)

1½ lbs. potatoes (old)   Pepper, salt
1½ ozs. butter

Peel a pound and a half of old potatoes, cut them into half-inch slices and put these into a saucepan with enough boiling salted water to cover them well. Boil, with the lid nearly closed, for from ten to fifteen minutes. Test with a knitting-needle; the potatoes should be soft, but not falling to pieces.

Drain, dry the saucepan and return the potatoes to it for a minute, setting it at the edge of the flame so that the potatoes may dry thoroughly.

Heat a little butter – about an ounce or rather over – in a frying-pan and when the butter is very hot add the slices of potato. Hold the frying-pan firmly over the flame with one hand and with the other chop the potatoes, using a long-handled knife. Don't chop the potatoes to a mash, but let no piece be left larger than the tip of your thumb. Shake well, to prevent the potatoes sticking, add plenty of salt and pepper and use the flat of your knife to press the potatoes into the shape of a flat cake, about half the size of the pan. Cover the pan with an *enamel* plate and leave it over a moderate flame until the potatoes begin to smoke – about five or seven minutes. By

153

this time the fat in the pan should have disappeared. With the help of a fish-slice, turn the cake of potatoes OVER and out on to the dish which is to hold the cutlets. The golden-brown underneath side will now appear uppermost.

RECIPE 4.
Runner Beans. (Cost: about 8½d.)

  2 lbs. runner beans.   Salt, pepper
     ½ oz. butter

Scarlet runners, when very young, are one of the most delightful of English vegetables, but when old they are apt to be too stringy for enjoyment. Buy two pounds, wash them and cut off the extreme rim of every bean all the way round. (Don't let any bean escape on the ground of supposed infancy – it is too risky, for one stringy bean will spoil a dish.) Cut each bean lengthwise into thin slices, or alternatively break it into short pieces with your hands.

Put the beans into a saucepan with plenty of boiling salted water and boil fairly fast with the lid off for fifteen minutes. Then test the beans, by eating one to see if it is tender. Look out, it will be hot. As soon as the beans are cooked, turn them out into a colander and drain them very thoroughly. Then put them into a hot vegetable dish with a little salt and pepper sprinkled over them and half an ounce of butter melting into them. Cover the dish with a dry, clean cloth and keep it hot.

RECIPE 5.
Milky Rice Pudding. (Cost: about 5½d.)

1½ ozs. rice	1 oz. butter
1 oz. castor sugar	Pinch of salt
1 pint milk	A little nutmeg, or vanilla

Children who screamed at the sight of rice pudding will sometimes, even often, grow up with a passion for it. If, however, it is still anathema, your guests can be consoled with cherries.

Wash an ounce and a half of rice (a tablespoonful and a quarter) and put it into a pie-dish with a pinch of salt and a tablespoonful of castor sugar. (Use Carolina rice, which is best for puddings – Patna and Java are good for curry.) Add a pint of milk and a grating of nutmeg, or a few drops of vanilla essence. Stir well with a wooden spoon.

Cut up an ounce of butter into three or four pieces and put it on top of the milk. Now put the pie-dish in a very slow oven and cook, uncovered, for two hours – not less, on any account, for a good milk pudding can never be made quickly.

At the end of the first ten minutes, open the oven and stir the pudding with a wooden spoon. Do this twice more at ten-minute intervals – you will then have stirred the pudding three times in the first half-hour. If you cannot be at hand to do this, no harm will come to the pudding; but this extra stirring makes it very creamy.

When the pudding is cooked a pale golden skin

should have formed on the top and the rice inside will be soft all through. The skin will not form until the last half hour or so, so don't worry if after one and a half hours the rice still looks undressed.

RECIPE 6.

Stewed Cherries. (Cost: about 11d.)

1 lb. cherries   4 ozs. castor sugar

Buy a pound of cherries – the very deep red kind, not the pale yellowish pink ones which are best eaten raw. Wash them well and take off the stalks.

Put four tablespoonfuls of castor sugar with a teacupful of water into a saucepan and bring to the boil, stirring with a wooden spoon. When the syrup boils, add the cherries and simmer them very, very gently for ten minutes, or until they are soft – but NOT bursting and disclosing their stones.

Turn out into a dish and let them get cold – unless, of course, you prefer them hot. They will take a long while to get really cold on a hot summer's day, so, unless you can cook them a few hours before dinner, you had better serve them hot.

SEVEN DINNERS FOR SUMMER

SHOPPING LIST

	s.	d.
Butcher.		
10 lamb cutlets from the neck (English) ...	2	6
(Or, if New Zealand)	(2	1)
Dairy.		
1 pint milk	0	3
Greengrocer.		
1½ lbs. old potatoes	0	2½
(1 bunch mint – optional)	(0	1)
2 lbs. runner beans	0	8
1 lb. cherries (cooking)	0	10
From Stock.		
Oil, for cutlets	0	0½
Parsley, for cutlets	0	0½
6 ozs. castor sugar (less, if no mint sauce) ...	0	1
3 ozs. butter, for potatoes, beans and pudding	0	3
1½ ozs. rice	0	0½
	4	11
(Or, with New Zealand lamb and mint sauce)	4	7

Nutmeg, or vanilla flavouring, negligible.

TIME-TABLE

DINNER AT EIGHT O'CLOCK

N.B. – If you are dining at a different time, calculate from the time-table the hour at which you will have to start your preparations and then alter the hands of the

kitchen clock to conform with the time-table. You will find this easier than making individual calculations over every item.

If the cherries are to be eaten cold, you must have them cooked at least three hours beforehand. If they are to be eaten hot, they are included in the time-table.

5 30   (Make mint sauce, if you are having it.)

5 45   *Light oven for rice pudding.*
       Make rice pudding.

6 0   *Start cooking pudding in oven at very low heat.*
       Peel potatoes, slice them.

6 10   *Stir pudding.*

LAY THE TABLE

6 20   *Stir pudding.*
       Start boiling salted water for potatoes.
       Prepare beans.

6 30   *Stir pudding.*
       Start boiling potatoes.
       Finish preparing beans, if not already done.
       Wash and dry parsley.

6 45   *Drain potatoes*, dry pan and return potatoes in pan
         to edge of flame, to dry. When dry, cover sauce-
         pan and leave at edge of stove.

PUT PLATES AND DISHES IN POSITION FOR HEATING. YOU HAVE NOW NOTHING TO DO FOR ABOUT HALF AN HOUR

7 15   *Start boiling salted water for beans.*
       Wash and stalk cherries.

7 20   *Start making syrup for cherries.*

7 25   *Start simmering cherries in syrup*, very gently.
       Start boiling beans, lid off.
       Prepare cutlets for grilling.

7 29   *Melt butter in frying-pan for potatoes.*

SEVEN DINNERS FOR SUMMER

7	30	*Start frying potatoes. Chop, press into shape.*
7	35	*Cover potatoes with plate, continue frying.*
7	36	*Remove cherries to edge of stove,* cover.
7	40	*Drain beans,* put in hot dish with butter, pepper, salt. Cover.
7	43	*Remove frying-pan with potatoes to edge of stove. Light grill.* Prepare cutlets for grilling.
7	50	*Start grilling cutlets at fierce heat.*
7	51	*Turn.*
7	52	*Lower heat of grill slightly, continue grilling.*
7	55	*Turn.*
7	57	Put cutlets on hot dish. Turn potatoes out of frying-pan on to same dish. Cover, put in bottom of oven.
8	0	Turn oven heat out. Leave rice pudding in oven. Take out dish with cutlets and potatoes, decorate with parsley.

Do not turn out cherries into dish until after the first course. Leave them, covered, in the saucepan near a low flame.

This is NOT A GOOD DINNER TO KEEP FOR LATECOMERS. The cutlets will get hard and the potatoes will lose crispness. The best you can do is to leave them in the oven, covered, with the heat turned as low as possible. Don't add parsley until the very last moment.

SALMON SOUFFLE

GARDEN PEAS

NEW POTATOES

HEARTS OF LETTUCE SALAD

RED CURRANT FOOL

SHORTBREAD FINGERS

RECIPE I.

Salmon *Soufflé*. (Cost: 2/– with sour milk; 2/6 with cream.)

   1 lb. chilled Canadian salmon OR 1 tin salmon
   2 eggs
   1 gill fresh milk
   1 gill sour milk OR 8d. worth cream
   2 ozs. flour
   1 oz. butter Pepper, salt

If you are using Canadian salmon, soak it in cold water for an hour, then cook it by putting it into a small saucepan of boiling salted water and boiling it gently for ten minutes. Strain it.

If you are using tinned salmon, open the tin and strain away the liquor.

In either case free the salmon from skin and bone and break it up into flakes with a silver fork (steel will give it an unpleasant flavour). It can be rubbed through a sieve, but this is rather a labour and not really necessary.

Make a panada (a *soufflé* foundation) by melting an ounce of butter in a saucepan, and when it is frothing, add two ounces of flour and blend thoroughly at the side of the fire. Then add very gradually the fresh milk, stirring it well in and keeping the mixture perfectly smooth. Return the saucepan to the fire and bring it slowly to the boil and stir until the mixture thickens and begins to leave the sides of the pan, making a ball in the centre. (This will be much thicker than a white sauce mixture, although the ingredients are the same.) Give it a final stir, and let it cool a little.

Meanwhile, beat up the eggs in separate basins. Then turn the cooled mixture from the saucepan into a basin and add the beaten eggs, one at a time, beating well all the time. Both the preliminary beating of the eggs and the beating in of them to the panada must be very thorough. It will take from ten to fifteen minutes.

Now add the salmon and stir it well in, then the sour milk or the cream. Season thoroughly with salt and pepper. Pour the mixture into a greased fireproof dish and put on the top of it a piece of greased paper which you have cut to the shape of the dish. A piece of paper which has wrapped up butter will have just the right amount of fat on it. Do not fasten it down, but just lay it lightly on top. This will prevent the top of the *soufflé* getting caked at all in the oven.

Bake for about forty minutes in a moderate oven. It should be served in the dish in which it was cooked.

RECIPE 2.
Garden Peas. (Cost: 6d.)

2 lbs. garden peas	1 teaspoonful sugar
A sprig of mint	Salt

Shell two pounds of peas and put them into boiling salted water with a little mint and a teaspoonful of sugar. Boil them very fast without a lid. After about fifteen minutes they should be cooked, but after they have been boiling for about twelve minutes the cook should begin dipping in a spoon and bringing out a few peas to taste. The moment they are done, they should be turned out of the saucepan, drained, the mint removed, and the peas put into a hot vegetable dish with butter, pepper and salt. It is very important that peas should not be overdone, and it is only by constant testing that the exact moment for taking them off the fire can be gauged.

Once the peas are cooked and drained, they will remain quite happily in the vegetable dish for a short time.

RECIPE 3.
New Potatoes. (Cost: about 3d.)

1½ lbs. new potatoes	A sprig of mint
Salt, pepper, butter	A little chopped parsley

Scrape the potatoes and put them into boiling salted water with a little mint. Boil with the lid half on for from fifteen to twenty minutes, and then test them very gently with a knitting-needle. As soon as they are soft, turn them into a colander to drain, and then put them into a hot vegetable dish with a little melted butter and sprinkle them with a little finely-chopped parsley. Keep the lid on.

(A good plan for buttering the potatoes is to cover them with the paper which was wrapped round half a pound of butter, or with an inverted butter dish from which nearly all the butter has been used.)

RECIPE 4.
Hearts of Lettuce Salad. (Cost: about 6d.)

1 or 2 lettuces	1 spring onion
Pepper, salt	French mustard
Olive oil	Tarragon vinegar or lemon juice

Take the crisp inside leaves of long or round lettuce – whichever you prefer, or whichever seems fresher in the shop on the day of purchase. Ignore any leaves which are blemished – to use them is a trifling economy and the results are disastrous.

Wash the leaves well by placing them in a colander in a bowl of water under a running tap. This ensures their being in a bath of running water without danger of their being floated out of the basin. Do not leave them to soak, but wash each leaf yourself, paying minute attention to every piece of lettuce. As soon as they are clean, put the colander in the sink and let the water run out; then put the lettuce leaves in a wire basket or a clean cloth and swing them around to dry them. Then with a clean dry

163

cloth dry each leaf yourself, just dabbing it lightly free from water. This is undoubtedly a bore, but your leaves *must not* be wet.

French Dressing.

Rub around a bowl with a spring onion. If you have a big wooden salad spoon use it to mix the dressing in. If you haven't, use a cup. Take a pinch of salt, a tiny pinch of pepper and a mustard spoonful of French mustard. Mix together with a tablespoonful of olive oil. Add half a tablespoonful of tarragon vinegar (this has a very special aniseed taste which some people dislike, but which most true salad lovers value) or lemon juice, still mixing. Finally, add a further half-tablespoonful of olive oil. Mix well. Put the salad leaves in the bowl rubbed with onion. Pour the dressing over the salad, and turn between two spoons until the lettuce is thoroughly coated with the dressing.

Then arrange the leaves neatly on plates and allow each person his individual lettuce leaves.

RECIPE 5.
Red Currant Fool. (Cost: about 1/4.)

1 lb. red currants	4 ozs. sugar
6d. worth cream	

Pick one pound of red currants from their stalks, and cook them very gently for about eight minutes in a syrup made of four ounces of castor sugar and a very little water – just enough to cover the bottom of the pan. Let them cool for a few moments, and then rub them through a sieve into a basin. Slightly whip the cream until it is thick enough to run in a ribbon when dropped from the spoon. Stir the cream into the red currant *purée* and pour this into custard glasses. Serve very cold.

RECIPE 6.
Shortbread Fingers. (Cost: 3d.)

2 ozs. butter	3 ozs. flour
A pinch of salt	1 oz. sugar

Sieve the flour and salt, and then rub the butter into the flour very thoroughly with the tips of the fingers. Then add the sugar. Turn out the mixture (which should look quite dry) on to a floured board and knead until it forms a ball of dough. It will need some perseverance to make sure that no cracks remain, but this must be done as quickly as possible. If it is bullied sufficiently, however, the unpromising heap of dry flour and butter will actually form a dough. Then quickly roll it out about half an inch thick on a floured board and cut it into small fingers about two inches long and rather less than an inch wide. (The above quantities will make eight to ten fingers.) Prick these all over with a fork, and put them on a greased baking sheet. Bake for about fifty minutes in a cool oven until they are light brown. Allow them to cool on the baking sheet for a few minutes before removing them to a cake-rack. Eat them warm – they are delicious. But they are, of course, perfectly good eaten cold.

DINNERS FOR BEGINNERS

SHOPPING LIST

						s.	d.
Fishmonger.							
1 lb. chilled Canadian salmon ...		...		...		1	6
(Or 1 tin at the same price)							
Dairy.							
2 eggs ...	...	...	...	...	...	0	3
½ pint milk (1 gill should be sour)			...		...	0	1½
3 ozs. butter ...	...	...	...	...	...	0	3
Cream (for fool) ...	...	...	...	...	...	0	6
Greengrocer.							
2 lbs. peas ...	...	...	...	...	...	0	6
1½ lbs. potatoes ...	...	...	...	...	...	0	3
1 or 2 lettuces ...	...	...	...	...	...	0	6
1 lb. red currants ...	...	...	...	...	...	0	10
Mint, parsley ...	...	...	...	...	...	0	1
From Stock.							
5 ozs. flour ...	...	...	...	...	...	0	1
Vinegar, olive oil, spring onion ...		...		...		0	0½
5 ozs. sugar ...	...	...	...	...	...	0	1
						5	0

TIME-TABLE

DINNER AT EIGHT O'CLOCK

N.B. – If you are dining at a different time, calculate from the time-table the hour at which you will have to start your preparations and then alter the hands of the kitchen clock to conform with the time-table. You will find it easier than making individual calculations over every item.

SEVEN DINNERS FOR SUMMER

As you have rather a large number of dishes to prepare, this meal takes extra time to cook. You can save forty minutes, however, by making the fool in the morning.

5 30 (or morning) Make red currant fool. This will take about 40 minutes, and then it will be off your mind. Leave in a very cool place.

6 10 Shell peas.
Scrape potatoes.

6 30 *Put salted water on to boil for salmon.*

6 35 *Light oven for shortbread* (make the oven moderate).
Put salmon in boiling water, to boil for ten minutes.
Make shortbread.

6 45 *Put shortbread in coolest part of oven.*
Make salmon soufflé – this will take about 30 minutes.

7 15 *Put salmon soufflé on top shelf of oven.*
LAY THE TABLE

7 30 *Put salted water on to boil for peas and potatoes.*
PUT PLATES AND DISHES TO HEAT

7 40 *Put on peas and potatoes to cook.*
Wash and dry lettuce.
Make salad dressing, coat lettuce, and arrange for table.

7 50 *Take shortbread out of oven and leave to cool on baking sheet.* Test peas and potatoes.

7 55 *Drain and dish up peas and potatoes, unless already done.*
Take salmon soufflé out of oven. Serve in the dish in which it was cooked.

If people are late, leave the salmon in the oven, covered, with the heat turned low. Leave peas and potatoes in their vegetable dishes on top of the oven. Leave lettuce and fool in the coolest possible place. This is not a good meal to keep waiting, but the salmon *soufflé* is not so frail as ordinary *soufflés*, and obligingly does not fall if kept back a little.

167

CHAPTER V

Autumn Menu No. 1   FOR FOUR PEOPLE

SQUAB PIE

CORN ON THE COB

BAKED PEARS

CORN on the cob – known to some people as 'mealies', to others as 'sweet corn' – is a delicacy that all who have been in America will gratefully remember. There it is supposed only to be eaten in perfection when it comes straight from the field to the kitchen. This ideal state of affairs cannot be hoped for in England, where, however, corn on the cob is sold in the greengrocers' in greater quantities every autumn. Every year it seems to be cheaper and to arrive in a fresher state. If you buy some with care, and cook and eat it in the way described here, you will get some idea of how good it can be.

Squab pie is a dish as typically English as corn on the cob is American. It comes from the West Country, where it has many variations.

RECIPE 1.

Squab Pie. (Cost: about 1/10½.)

    1 lb. stewing steak, or middle neck of New Zealand
       Lamb
    1 lb. onions
    ½ bundle leeks
    1 lb. potatoes
    1 lb. cooking apples
    2 ozs. brown sugar
    ½ gill water
    Salt, pepper

Buy a pound of middle neck of New Zealand lamb
or, alternatively, of stewing steak. Mutton is the best
meat in flavour for this dish; beef, on the other hand,
is easier to handle and more economical, owing to
the absence of bone and superfluous gristle and fat.
Choose which you like.

Wipe your meat and trim away superfluous skin,
fat, etc. If it is beef, cut it up into inch-square pieces.
Put the meat in the bottom of a deep fireproof dish.

Peel and quarter a pound of onions. Wash and
peel a pound of potatoes, and cut them into slices
about an eighth of an inch thick, which you dry in a
cloth. Cut any dark or damaged top leaves from half
a bundle of leeks, leaving only the white stalk and
pale yellowish green lower part of the leaves. Wash
them thoroughly free from grit, and cut them in
two-inch lengths.

Cover the meat with a layer of mixed onions, leeks
and potatoes. Sprinkle with plenty of salt and

pepper. Add half a teacupful of water, cover the dish with the lid and cook in a slow oven for an hour and a half.

At the end of this time, add a pound of apples, peeled, cored and cut in quarters, and two tablespoonfuls of brown sugar. Cover again, return to the oven and go on cooking slowly as before for another forty minutes.

(2 hours and 10 minutes in the oven.)
Serve in the dish in which it was cooked.

RECIPE 2.
Corn on the Cob. (Cost about 2/–.)

| 4 heads green corn | Pepper, salt, butter |

Buy one cob for each person. Before you buy them turn back the green husk and the silky fibre below it and examine the grain of the cob. It should be the palest yellow and evenly graduated from small grains at the ends to grains of about the size of a pea in the centre. Don't buy the corn if the grains are brown or uneven. If the greengrocer objects to your examining the corn by turning back the husk, then take the cob in your hand and press it gently. If you can feel a faintly springy resistance to the pressure of your fingers through the husk, then the corn will not be too old.

Remove the husk and the silky tassel of fibre from the corn, cut off any extra stalk at the bottom, and cook in boiling salted water with the lid off for about twenty-five minutes. Boil fast, and see that there is enough water to cover the cobs completely. Test to see whether the corn is cooked by lifting up one cob and picking off a grain. IT WILL BE HOT. Eat it; it should be almost as tender as a young pea. When the cobs are cooked, drain them thoroughly in the colander. All moisture should be allowed to evaporate from them. Wrap them in a warm napkin to keep them hot and place the napkin in a hot dish.

Serve the corn as a separate course, for it will demand all the eater's attention. Each guest should take a cob to himself. He must hold it in one hand, spread a generous allowance of butter along one row of grain from end to end and then sprinkle the row with salt and pepper. He should then hold the cob at each end and nibble along the row from one end to the other – not round and round the cob. As he finishes each row, he should butter the next and so on until all is finished. The whole affair is a bit of an orgy, but worth it. It would be wise to provide finger-bowls of hot water with the corn.

RECIPE 3.
Baked Pears. (Cost: about 1/0½.)

> 4 large or 8 small stewing pears
> 3 ozs. brown sugar
> 4d. worth cream

The success of this simple and delicious dish depends upon its long, slow cooking in the oven.

Buy four large or eight small stewing pears. Take the stalks off, wipe the pears, but do not peel them, and prick them deeply in several places with a long darning-needle. Put half an inch of water with three tablespoonfuls of brown sugar (and a tablespoonful or two of black currant or blackberry jelly, if you have any open in the house) into a saucepan and stir with a wooden spoon until the sugar melts. Then pour it into a fireproof dish, stand the pears in the syrup and cook very, very slowly in the oven, at the lowest possible heat, for four hours. Do not cover. The pears should turn dark, dark brown (almost purplish) and become slightly wrinkled, while the syrup in which they stand will be almost a glaze. Baste them with this syrup from time to time – that is, pour it over the pears with a spoon.

When the pears are cooked, whip up fourpenny-worth of cream until it is very slightly thickened and pour it into the syrup in the bottom of the dish.

Serve the pears either hot or cold, whichever you prefer, in the dish in which they were cooked. Eat the skins; it would be the very madness of refinement to set them aside.

SEVEN DINNERS FOR AUTUMN

SHOPPING LIST

Butcher.						s.	d.
1 lb. stewing steak, or middle neck of New Zealand mutton						1	2

Dairy.
Cream	0	4

Greengrocer.
1 lb. potatoes	0	1½
1 lb. onions	0	1½
½ bundle leeks	0	3
1 lb. cooking apples	0	3
4 heads of corn	2	0
4 large or 8 small stewing pears (about 2 lbs.) ...	0	8

From Stock.
6 ozs. brown sugar	0	1
	5	0

TIME-TABLE

DINNER AT EIGHT O'CLOCK

N.B. – If you are dining at a different time, calculate from the time-table the hour at which you will have to start your preparations and then alter the hands of the kitchen clock to conform with the time-table. You will find this easier than making individual calculations over every item.

Start the pears at ten minutes to four. Preparing them and making the syrup will not take more than ten minutes;

173

put them in the top of the oven at very low heat, and you need then do nothing, except baste them occasionally, until 5.30, when you should start upon the squab pie.

5 30   Trim and cut up meat for squab pie.
       Prepare potatoes.
5 40   Turn oven up very slightly. Prepare onions.
       Prepare leeks.
5 50   *Put pears on lower shelf of oven, start cooking squab pie on top shelf.*

YOU ARE NOW FREE FOR AN HOUR AND TWENTY MINUTES, EXCEPT FOR AN OCCASIONAL BASTING OF THE PEARS

LAY THE TABLE

7 10   Peel, core and quarter apples.
7 20   *Add apples and sugar to squab pie,* continue cooking as before.
7 25   *Start boiling salted water for corn.*
       Prepare corn.

PUT PLATES AND DISHES TO WARM IN BOTTOM OF OVEN OR ON RACK COVERED WITH CLOTH. WARM NAPKIN FOR CORN

7 35   Start boiling corn.
7 55   Whip cream slightly, take pears out of oven and add cream to syrup. Leave in warm place.
8 0   *Drain corn.* Wrap in hot napkin and put in warm dish. Take out squab pie.

If people are late, the squab pie can remain in the oven. Turn heat down as low as possible. The corn can remain wrapped in the napkin. It retains its heat for a long time.

CHICKEN BAKED IN MILK
BRAISED CELERY
CHEESE POTATOES

SUNSHINE CREAM

This is a very good meal to serve when you want to have a free afternoon and evening, because everything in it (except the sweet, which is cold) goes into the oven at about half-past two and remains there, without any need for supervision, until eight o'clock (or even later, if you are delayed). It leaves you free to greet early arrivals and is an ideal week-end meal when guests are in the house; moreover, when the time comes to eat it, it is very good. Although the food takes so long to cook, it is not expensive, for the heat is kept very low indeed all the time. Altogether this meal deserves a special little halo of its own.

If you are cooking the whole menu, be careful to

arrange the food in the oven so that the chicken and vegetables are cooked at the same speed. All should be in the uppermost part of the oven; anything in the lower half of such a cool oven would hardly be cooked at all.

RECIPE 1.

Chicken Baked in Milk. (Cost: about 3/5.)

1 boiling fowl	2 ozs. butter
1 pint milk	2 ozs. flour
	Pepper, salt

Ask your poulterer for a boiling fowl, weighing about three and a half pounds. Let it be as old, and therefore cheap, as you like; age and toughness will yield to the long, slow cooking. Ask the poulterer to joint your fowl for you. This means cutting it up into two leg portions, two wings, two breast fillets, and the merry-thought part of the neck. If the poulterer will not do this, or if you are buying the fowl from a farmer who does nothing beyond cleaning and plucking, you can quite easily joint the bird yourself with a sharp knife. A demonstration is the ideal way of learning, but the following description may help you.

To Joint a Chicken.

Use a pair of scissors to cut the skin. Put a sharp pointed knife between the leg of the chicken and the side, and cut through the joint. You will find it easier, as an amateur, to do this if you first cut away the skin round the joint with the scissors. The skin

176

is quite loose and will come away easily, revealing more of the bird's anatomy.

Cut off both legs, and in similar fashion cut off the wings – find the joint by exploring with your finger outside the bird. Cut right through the gristly part between joint and socket.

Next make an incision just above the merry-thought bone again, feeling for it first with your fingers if you are not sure which end it is. Turn back the merry-thought and neck-bones and cut them off.

Next cut the breast away from each side of the bone, making two fillets.

Finally, whether you jointed the chicken yourself or had it done for you, remove as much skin from the bird as possible. The less skin there is, the better eating this dish will be. Remove fat also; this, in an uncooked bird, is yellow and easily recognisable.

Warm a pint of milk in a saucepan.

Sift two tablespoonfuls of flour on to an enamel plate and season it with a teaspoonful of salt and half a teaspoonful of pepper.

Now heat two ounces of butter in a large saucepan. When the butter is sizzling and frothing, put in the joints of chicken and sear them quickly over a fierce heat. This will only take a few seconds; the chicken will brown very slightly on the outside and turn whitish inside almost at once. Lift out the pieces with a fish-slice (leaving the saucepan near the flame but not directly over it), roll them in the seasoned flour and pack them tightly into a fireproof dish.

Shake all the surplus flour from the plate into the remaining hot butter in the saucepan (the flour should amount to about a level tablespoonful – if it does not, add some more) and stir it vigorously into the butter with a wooden spoon. Add, very gradually, your pint of warm milk, still stirring busily all the time. When all the milk is added, continue simmering and stirring for from five to seven minutes. The consistency of this mixture should be less thick than that of a white sauce – about that of a thin custard. Taste and season. Pour it over the chicken, which should completely disappear beneath it. Close the lid of the fireproof dish tightly and bake in the slowest possible oven for five and a half hours.

When the dish is cooked the milk will appear as a creamy golden-brown gravy and the chicken will be so tender that it can almost be taken from the bones with a spoon.

RECIPE 2.
Braised Celery. (Cost: about 3½d.)

| 1 head celery | 1 oz. butter | Pepper, salt |

Buy a large head of celery and break the sticks from the root one by one. Discard any sticks which will not break almost clean in two. The slow braising will render any but the most fibrous sticks tender, but it is no use hoping that anything on earth will make the very tough outside portions of an old head of celery eatable.

Wash the celery under the tap, using a brush to get

off every scrap of earth and grit. Cut up into pieces
about two inches long.

Melt an ounce of butter in a saucepan. When the
butter is melted and very hot put in the celery and
turn it about a little, as you fry it, for two minutes.
Shake the pan, so that the celery does not brown.
When it is fried, put it into a fireproof dish, add
pepper and salt and pour over any butter remaining
in the saucepan. Shake well, with the lid on, so that
the butter is distributed all over the celery. Keep the
lid on and put the dish in the oven to cook for five
and a half hours at the same low heat as the fowl.

RECIPE 3.
Cheese Potatoes. (Cost: about 4d.)

| 1 lb. potatoes | 2 ozs. cooking cheese |
| ½ pint milk | Pepper, salt |

This way of cooking potatoes fits in with the long-
period cooking that is being employed for the rest
of the meal.

Peel a pound of potatoes and cut them into slices
about a quarter of an inch thick. Rinse these slices
in cold water, dry them in a cloth and put a layer
in the bottom of a fireproof dish. Sprinkle with
pepper and salt and a layer of grated cheese.
(Though gruyère and parmesan are excellent cooking cheeses, they are expensive, and you will do
well instead to use either kraft or cheddar, both of
which are cheap, keep dry, and are therefore easy
to grate, and have an excellent flavour.) Follow this

with another layer of potatoes, seasoning and grated cheese, and so on until your potatoes are used up. The top layer must be of cheese and rather thicker than the preceding cheese layers. Pour half a pint of milk gently into the side of the dish, taking care not to wash the cheese from the top as you do so. If your dish is not very deep you will not need so much as half a pint of milk.

Do not cover, but put in the oven and bake for five and a half hours with the other dishes. Be careful with this, as with the others, not to put it too low down in the oven to get sufficient heat.

RECIPE 4.

Sunshine Cream. (Cost: about 1/1½.)

5 eggs	½ lb. castor sugar
	2 lemons

This is a most delicate and even grand-looking sweet and at the same time very easy and straightforward to make. It is eaten cold, and should be made at least three hours before dinner is ready. In this instance, we propose making it six hours before dinner, in order to fit it in with the scheme of the free afternoon and evening.

Take two basins. Separate the yolks of five eggs from the whites by cracking each egg against the edge of a basin and letting the white drip down into the basin while you turn the yolk from one half of the shell to the other until it is free of white. Put all the yolks in the second basin.

Beat the yolks with a beater or a fork for a minute

until they are frothing. Then add the strained juice of two lemons (about four good tablespoonfuls of lemon juice). Stir with a wooden spoon. Add half a pound (a breakfastcupful) of castor sugar and stir again.

Fill the lower part of a double boiler with water and set it to heat while you beat up the five whites. Beat them with a fork or whisk until they are stiff enough to pile into a peak. This will not take less than ten minutes' hard beating, possibly fifteen. When they are pure white and very stiff, set them aside in a cool place while you cook the yolks and lemon. The water in the double boiler should by now be boiling.

Pour the egg and lemon mixture into the top half of the boiler and stir steadily in one direction with a wooden spoon until the mixture thickens to the consistency of thick cream. It will take about ten minutes and during this time you must give it all your attention.

When the mixture thickens, turn it out into a large clean basin and fold in the stiffly-beaten whites. To do this, add the whites gradually, in about five instalments, and as each bit of frothed white falls into the yellow, lift the latter over and round it with the flat side of a pastry-knife. Continue in this way, not stirring round and round, but lifting over and over, until the white is taken right into the yellow and can no longer be seen separately.

It is very important that all the yellow and white

should be completely blended. If not, the yellow will turn hard and glossy and the white will sink into a watery substance at the bottom of the glass. Therefore, make sure that your knife goes right to the bottom of the basin each time and that no streak of white remains anywhere in the mixture.

This sweet, when perfectly blended, should form a pale yellow froth, ineffably light, yet firm enough to pile into glasses. There should be enough to fill five or six moderately large grapefruit glasses.

Set aside to cool. The sweet will keep its original appearance and taste for a day or two.

SHOPPING LIST

	s.	d.
Poulterer.		
1 boiling fowl, weighing 3½ lbs	3	0
Dairy.		
¼ lb. butter	0	3
1½ pints milk (or rather less may be wanted) ...	0	4½
5 eggs	0	10
Greengrocer.		
2 lemons	0	2
1 lb. potatoes	0	1½
1 head celery	0	2½
From Stock.		
½ lb. castor sugar	0	1½
2 ozs. cooking cheese	0	1
	5	2

Flour, negligible.

SEVEN DINNERS FOR AUTUMN

TIME-TABLE

Dinner at Eight O'Clock

N.B. – If you are dining at a different time, calculate from the time-table the hour at which you will have to start your preparations and then alter the hands of the kitchen clock to conform with the time-table. You will find it easier than making individual calculations over every item.

———

You can make the sweet either before or after the rest of the meal has been put in the oven. If you want to keep the whole afternoon and evening free from cooking, then make the sweet in the morning or even on the previous day. It must be finished at least three hours (less in cold weather) before dinner-time.

We will suppose that you are making the sweet before starting to prepare the rest of the meal.

12 50	Separate yolks and whites of eggs.
	Mix yolks with lemon and sugar and set aside.
12 56	*Start heating water in double boiler.*
12 57	Whip whites.
1 10	Put whites in cool place.
	Put yolks, lemon, etc., in top of double boiler, cook and stir for ten minutes or until thickened.
1 20	*Turn yolk mixture into basin and fold in whites.*
1 25	Put mixture into glasses and set aside to cool.

Wash Up

1 30	Joint your fowl. This may take as long as half an hour if you are inexperienced – if you are accustomed to it, not more than ten minutes.
2 0	*Warm pint of milk.*
	Prepare seasoned flour on plate.

2	05	*Heat butter and fry pieces of chicken.*
		When finished, leave saucepan with butter near, but not on flame.
2	08	Roll pieces of chicken in seasoned flour and pack in casserole.
2	10	*Light oven.*
		Add remainder of seasoned flour to butter and make thin sauce with addition of warm milk.
2	20	*Pour sauce over chicken. Cover dish tightly and put in oven – on a shelf half-way up, or higher.*
2	22	Wash and cut up celery.
		Peel, slice, rinse and dry potatoes.
2	35	*Melt butter in frying-pan. Lightly fry celery.*
2	43	*Put celery in casserole with pepper and salt, pour butter over, cover and put in oven – top shelf.*
2	45	Put potatoes in fireproof dish with butter, seasoning and grated cheese. Pour in milk.
		Put potatoes in oven side by side with celery, if possible.

If people are late the dinner can continue cooking without coming to harm for another half-hour or so. All food is sent to table in the dishes in which it was cooked so there is nothing for you to do before dinner but warm the plates (in the bottom half of the oven) and lay the table.

POACHER'S RABBIT
CAULIFLOWER MOULD

AUTUMN PUDDING (BLACKBERRY)
JUNKET AND CREAM

Don't despise rabbit because it is cheap. Country people know how to cook it in a dozen delicious ways, and here is one of them.

Autumn pudding is a new version of an old favourite – summer pudding – which is made in the same way, but with raspberries and red currants in place of blackberries. Either cream or custard is very good with this pudding, but junket is chosen here instead because, like rabbit, it is often condemned as something commonplace and rather dreary. Actually, when well made, it is one of our most excellent English dishes.

RECIPE 1.
Poacher's Rabbit. (Cost: about 3/-.)

1 English rabbit	1 bunch parsley
4 rashers bacon	1 bay leaf
¼ lb. mushrooms	4 tablespoonfuls vinegar
1 lb. onions	Nutmeg
1 lb. potatoes	Pepper, salt

Buy an English rabbit weighing two pounds and

ask the butcher or poulterer to skin it, clean it and cut it up for you. Wash it and leave it to soak in a bowl of cold water with a little salt until you want to cook it, letting it soak for an hour at least.

Wipe, peel and chop coarsely a quarter of a pound of mushrooms. Wash, dry and chop a bunch of parsley. Peel and slice a pound of onions. Wash and peel a pound of potatoes; cut them lengthwise into slices about an eighth of an inch thick, and dry them in a cloth.

Put a bay leaf in the bottom of a large deep fireproof dish. Cut the rind from four rashers of fat bacon with a pair of scissors.

Now dry the pieces of rabbit in a cloth, cut them, if you like, into smaller or more equal sized pieces, rub them with plenty of pepper and salt and a little grated nutmeg. Set the head aside for stock.

Put a layer of rabbit in the bottom of the fireproof dish, then a layer of mushrooms, onions and parsley, then another layer of rabbit and so on until you have used up all these things. Season each layer. Cover the top with a thick layer of the sliced potatoes. Sprinkle over four tablespoonfuls of wine vinegar and lay the four rashers of bacon across the top of everything.

Put on the lid, close it down firmly and cook for two hours in a quick oven.

Don't Take off the Lid to see how Things are getting on, no matter how exciting the smell may be.

Serve in the dish in which it was cooked.

RECIPE 2.
Cauliflower Mould. (Cost: about 8d.)

1 cauliflower	About a gill of milk
1 oz. butter	A little nutmeg
1 oz. flour	Pepper, salt, paprika

Buy a medium-sized cauliflower with a clean, un-damaged face. If the surrounding leaves are firm in texture and the stalks have a greenish-grey bloom, then the cauliflower is really fresh. Strip off any damaged leaves and leave the cauliflower to soak in cold water with a handful of salt to draw out hidden insects. Put the cauliflower head downwards in the water.

To prepare for cooking, break off the leaves, wash them, and set any small ones aside. You will now see where the 'flowers', each on its own stalk, join the main stem. Cut off the separate stems with their flowers and wash them again under cold, running water.

Put plenty of water with a handful of salt to boil in a saucepan, and when it boils add the flowers and leaves which you have drained of water. Cook fairly fast with the lid off until tender – about fifteen minutes, but test for yourself and see. Don't cook it until the flowers begin to fall to pieces. Drain thoroughly.

The moment you begin to cook the cauliflower, you must start on the sauce which is to cover it. Melt an ounce of butter in a saucepan and when it

187

is melted and very hot add a tablespoonful of flour, and work it into the butter. Take the saucepan to the edge of the stove and add, little by little, rather more than a small teacupful of warm milk, stirring hard as you go. When the mixture is stirred quite smooth, add nearly a teacupful of the water in which the cauliflower is boiling and stir again until smooth. This will take about ten minutes altogether. Now grate in a little nutmeg and put the saucepan back on the flame; let the sauce simmer for five minutes more, keep on stirring. After five minutes you must set it at the edge of the stove again, as you have to drain the cauliflower. Taste and season, if necessary, but remember there is a lot of salt in the cauliflower water.

Butter the inside of a small pudding basin while the cauliflower is draining. Put each of the drained 'flowers', head downwards, into this basin, and pack them until all are in. Fill in any space that is left with the leaves, chopped up roughly, and with any flowers that have been broken in cooking. When everything is in, press it down well with a plate and turn it out into a hot vegetable dish. Stir the sauce and simmer it for another minute, then pour it over the cauliflower mould. Put the lid on and set the dish on the plate-rack with a flame below – in this way it will remain hot for a long time. At the last moment, before serving, dust the cauliflower over with paprika.

RECIPE 3.

Autumn Pudding. (Cost: about 7½d.)

    1 lb. blackberries   4 tablespoonfuls castor sugar
    1 gill water   Slices of white bread
    Slice or two of lemon peel

Buy a pound of blackberries – fat, black ones, not those that look withered or reddish in colour. Wash them with care and pick them over, rejecting insects, stalks and unripe fruit.

Put the blackberries into a saucepan with four tablespoonfuls of castor sugar, a slice or two of dried lemon peel to bring out the flavour of the fruit, and a teacupful of water. Bring slowly to the boil, stirring occasionally, and cook gently for about ten minutes – say twenty minutes at the most altogether. Pick out a blackberry (IT WILL BE HOT) and see if it is thoroughly cooked.

While the blackberries are cooking you must keep an eye on them, but it will be possible at the same time to prepare the rest of the pudding. Cut fairly thin slices of bread from a white loaf and cut off the crusts (which you can dry in the oven for crumbs). Line a pudding basin with the slices so that the bottom and sides are completely covered. When the blackberries are cooked, pour them straight into this lined basin – do not be alarmed by the amount of juice, as a great deal of it will be absorbed by the bread. Put a weight on a plate on top of the basin and leave it in a cool place to get thoroughly cold.

189

To serve, turn out the pudding into a glass dish. If there is difficulty in turning it out, run a pastry-knife round the edges of the basin. The juice should run out round the pudding – do not worry if it collapses a little, as this only means that you have too much juice. This may not look well, but it is better than producing a dry and stodgy mass of bread.

RECIPE 4.
Junket and Cream. (Cost: about 7d.)

1 pint milk	1 tablespoonful castor sugar
1 dessertspoonful rennet	4d. worth cream

Heat a pint of milk very gently in a saucepan. Add a tablespoonful of castor sugar, which you must stir until it dissolves. When the milk is at blood-heat dip in your finger, it should feel neither hot nor cold, but just comfortable; take the saucepan away from the stove and pour into it a full dessertspoonful of rennet. Give the milk one good stir round after adding the rennet and pour it immediately into whatever you mean to serve it in – either a glass dish or separate grapefruit glasses. Leave to set in a cool place.

Just before serving pour fourpennyworth of cream unwhipped and unsweetened, over the junket. Have *brown sugar* on the table to accompany the junket.

SHOPPING LIST

	s.	d.
Butcher or Poulterer.		
1 English rabbit (about 2 lbs.) skinned, cleaned and chopped	1	8
Dairy.		
Cream	0	4
1 pint of milk (for junket)	0	3
Greengrocer.		
¼ lb. mushrooms	0	6
1 bunch parsley	0	1
1 lb. onions	0	1½
1 lb. potatoes	0	1½
1 medium cauliflower	0	6
1 lb. blackberries	0	6
From Stock.		
4 rashers of bacon (fat)	0	5
1 oz. butter (for cauliflower)	0	1
Milk for cauliflower	0	1
Vinegar	0	1
5 ozs. sugar	0	1
Bread for pudding	0	0½
Flour, nutmeg, paprika, rennet, lemon-peel, negligible		
	4	10½

TIME-TABLE

Dinner at Eight O'Clock

N.B. – If you are dining at a different time, calculate from the time-table the hour at which you will have to start your preparations and then alter the hands of the

kitchen clock to conform with the time-table. You will find it easier than making individual calculations over every item.

———

Put the cauliflower and the pieces of rabbit to soak in cold salted water until they are wanted.

If possible, make the blackberry pudding and junket in the morning. They will only take three-quarters of an hour altogether to cook. In any case, if you can manage it, you should have them prepared three hours before dinner, as fruit holds heat for a long time and the blackberry pudding should not be served up in a lukewarm state. Warm junket, too, is an abomination; see that yours is as cold as you can make it.

5 30 Wipe, peel and chop mushrooms.
   Peel potatoes, slice and dry.
   Wash and dry and chop parsley.
   Peel and chop onions.
5 50 *Light oven.*
   Dry pieces of rabbit, cut into size required, and rub with salt, pepper and a very little grated nutmeg.
   Put all ingredients into pie dish. Season.
6 0 *Start cooking rabbit in fast oven.*

  THERE IS NOTHING TO DO NOW FOR AN HOUR

7 0   LAY TABLE
7 15 *Start boiling salted water for cauliflower.*
   Prepare cauliflower by cutting off 'flowers'.

  PUT PLATES AND DISHES TO WARM IN RACK

7 25 *Start boiling cauliflower.*
   Start making white sauce.

7 40   *Set sauce at edge of stove.*
       Turn out cauliflower and drain.
       Grease bowl.
       Fill bowl with cauliflower, press down and turn out into
          hot vegetable dish.
7 50   (about) *Stir sauce, simmer for a minute, pour over*
          cauliflower, cover dish and leave on rack with small
          flame directly below.
7 55   Turn out blackberry pudding.
       Pour cream over junket.
8 0   Dust cauliflower with paprika.

If people are late you need not worry. The cauliflower
will remain unharmed where it is. Turn down the oven as
low as possible and leave the rabbit in the bottom. If you
are afraid that your pudding is very wet and may collapse,
do not turn it out at 7.55, but leave it where it is until the
moment when you want to serve it. Turning it out only
takes a few seconds. Do not dust paprika over cauliflower
until just before serving.

SAUSAGES AND KIDNEYS A LA TURBIGO

MASHED POTATOES

SAVOURY LEEKS

ORANGE CARAMEL

RECIPE I.

Sausages and and Kidneys *à la Turbigo.* (Cost: about
2/5½.)

1 lb. Chippolata sausages	1 onion
4 sheep's kidneys	½ oz. butter
¼ lb. mushrooms	Pepper, salt
½ lb. tomatoes	

Buy a pound of chippolata sausages, and four
large (chilled) sheep's kidneys. Skin, split and core the
kidneys, and rub them on both sides with pepper
and salt. Now cut them into thin slices. Throw away
the skin, but keep the cores, with any portions of
kidney adhering to them.

Wipe half a pound of ripe tomatoes, cut them into
quarters and put them in a saucepan with an onion
peeled and chopped, half an ounce of butter, two
cores of the kidneys, a teaspoonful of salt, and
nearly half a teaspoonful of pepper (this sauce must
be highly seasoned). Add a tablespoonful of water.

Cover the saucepan and simmer gently while you cook the sausages, kidneys and mushrooms. Light the oven, and warm a fairly shallow fireproof dish without a lid.

Prick the sausages with a fork in several places, and fry them in their own fat (if this is insufficient, add a little lard) until they are a nice brown colour on every side. This will take about ten minutes. Meanwhile you can wipe, peel and slice the mushrooms into fairly thin slices. Peel the stalks also and put them on an enamel plate in the bottom of the oven to dry. When they are dried you can store them in a tin with a good fitting lid and keep them for seasoning.

When the sausages are cooked, lift them out, drain them and cut them into fairly thick slices. Then put them in the fireproof dish which you have been warming for them. Close down the lid, and place the dish in the oven to keep warm, turning down the oven heat as low as possible.

Now fry the sliced kidneys and mushrooms in the fat left in the saucepan by the sausages (adding more lard if necessary). Fry them for about eight minutes, then lift them out, drain them well and place them in the fireproof dish with the sausages.

Take a look at the tomato sauce, stir it and squash it with a wooden spoon. If the tomatoes seem thoroughly cooked, put a colander over a large bowl and pour the contents of the saucepan into the colander. Take the *purée* that drains through and pour it over the sausages, kidneys and mushrooms in the fire-proof dish. Do not cover the dish again, but cook in the oven, uncovered, at low heat for half an hour longer.

Serve in the dish in which it was cooked.

RECIPE 2.
Mashed Potatoes. (Cost: about 2½d.)

1 lb. potatoes	½ gill milk
½ oz. butter	Pepper, salt

Peel a pound of potatoes, put them into a saucepan of cold water with a tablespoonful of salt and bring to the boil. Boil, with the lid almost closed, for about twenty minutes. Test the potatoes with a knitting-needle. When they are soft, drain them, dry the pan and return the potatoes to it for a minute. Set the pan near the flame so that the potatoes may be thoroughly dried. Now add about half a teacupful, or rather less, of warm milk (it is best warm, but cold will do if you are lazy or hurried), half an ounce of butter, a teaspoonful of salt and a good sprinkling of pepper. Mash all together with a fork and do it thoroughly – go on mashing for at least a minute longer than you think is necessary, for the whole point of potato *purée* is that it should be absolutely smooth and almost frothing with lightness, not a grey, dry mixture of lumps.

Serve piled in a hot vegetable dish.

RECIPE 3.
Savoury Leeks. (Cost: about 8d.)

1 bundle leeks	Pinch of herbs
2 tomatoes	2 ozs. butter
1 onion	

Buy a bundle of leeks, cut off any damaged leaves and the top of the green part, leaving only the white stalk and the tender greenish part of the leaves above. (Keep the leaves, if they are in good condition, for flavouring soup, etc.) Cut each leek in half and wash it well in cold water so as to clear it completely of grit (which is apt to lurk perseveringly in leeks).

Boil a saucepan of water with a tablespoonful of salt and a teaspoonful of vinegar. Cook the leeks in the boiling water with the lid of the saucepan off, for five minutes, then take them out and drain them.

While the leeks are cooking, heat two ounces of butter in a saucepan and when it is very hot, add two tomatoes, peeled and coarsely chopped, an onion peeled and cut in quarters, a pinch of herbs tied up in muslin, and a sprinkling of pepper and salt. (Pour a little boiling water over the tomatoes or dip them in the boiling water with the leeks, and they will skin quite easily.) When the leeks are drained, add them to the other vegetables in the saucepan, close down the lid tightly, and let all cook very gently for about forty minutes. Don't add any water if you can possibly help it, but if there should arise a smell of burning from the saucepan, then you may be forced to add a tablespoonful of stock if you have any, or some more butter – think of water only as a last resort. Actually, the vegetables should yield enough moisture to cook in the butter without any tendency to burn, but, if you keep your heat too high, burning may be the result.

Serve in a hot vegetable dish. Take out the herbs before serving and pour any liquid from the bottom of the saucepan over the vegetables.

RECIPE 4.
Orange Caramel. (Cost: about 1/7.)

  4 large oranges or 6 smaller ones
  2 ozs. lump sugar
  3 ozs. brown sugar
  6d. worth cream
  2 tablespoonfuls water.

Take four very large juicy oranges, or six smaller ones. Wash them, dry them and cut some thin slices with a sharp knife from the outer skin. Put these in a saucepan. With the same sharp knife peel the oranges, outer and inner skin together, allowing any juice that escapes to fall into the saucepan with the thin slices of rind. Cut carefully between all the dividing sections of skin in each orange so that the sections of orange are sliced out neatly, keeping their shape. Put the sections in a glass dish, remove any pips, and drain off any juice, adding it to the rind and juice in the saucepan. Add two tablespoonfuls of brown sugar and half a teacupful of water to the contents of the saucepan and simmer them gently for about fifteen minutes, so as to make a strong orange syrup.

While this syrup is cooking, make a caramel. Put two ounces of lump sugar and two tablespoonfuls of water in a saucepan and shake until the sugar boils into a thickish caramel. This will take about ten minutes, but you MUST watch it, as the final stages are very rapid. The syrup will throw up a lot of bubbles and turn yellowish-brown. As soon as it is a dark yellowish-brown, take the saucepan away from the flame and pour the caramel into a greased baking tin. Leave it to cool and set, then lever it out of the tin (turn the tin upside down and run hot water over it if this is difficult) and crush it with a rolling-pin.

Sprinkle a tablespoonful of brown sugar over the orange sections in the glass dish. Strain the orange syrup, keep back a tablespoonful and pour the rest over the sections in the dish. Whip up sixpennyworth of cream stiffly with a fork or whisk, and flavour it with the teaspoonful of orange syrup that you kept back. Now scatter the crushed caramel over the orange salad, and pile the whipped cream on top, or, if you prefer, hand it separately in a little dish.

You may prepare the oranges, the syrup and the caramel as early as you like, but do not put them all together until just before dinner.

Serve the orange caramel in separate glasses, one for each person, if you prefer.

SHOPPING LIST

		s.	d.
Butcher.			
4 sheep's kidneys (chilled)		1	0
Poulterer (or Grocer).			
1 lb. Chippolata sausages		1	4
Dairy.			
¼ lb. butter		0	3
Cream		0	6
Greengrocer.			
¼ lb. mushrooms		0	6
¾ lb. tomatoes		0	4
1 bundle leeks		0	4
1 lb potatoes		0	1½
4 large oranges, or 6 smaller ones		1	0
From Stock.			
2 onions		0	1
Milk for potatoes, about ½ gill or less		0	0½
Sugar for sweet, about 5 ozs.		0	1
Herbs	negligible		
		5	7

TIME-TABLE

DINNER AT EIGHT O'CLOCK

N.B. – If you are dining at a different time, calculate from the time-table the hour at which you will have to start your preparations and then alter the hands of the kitchen clock to conform with the time-table. You will find this easier than making individual calculations over every item.

---

5 30   Prepare oranges, make syrup and caramel. Strain syrup and leave to cool. Leave caramel to set.

6 0   LAY THE TABLE

6 10   Peel potatoes.

Prepare tomatoes. Wipe and quarter ½ lb. for sauce.

Peel and chop 2 (for savoury leeks).

Prepare onions. Peel and chop 1 (for sauce). Peel and quarter 1 (for savoury leeks).

Clean and cut up leeks.

Wipe, peel and slice mushrooms.

Tie up pinch of herbs in muslin.

Skin, split and core kidneys. Slice.

Prick sausages.

6 45   *Start boiling salted water for leeks.*

Start cooking tomatoes with butter, onion, kidney trimmings and seasoning in closed saucepan.

6 55   *Light oven,* put fireproof dish to warm.

Start boiling leeks.

Start frying sausages.

6 58   *Put butter to heat for leeks in saucepan.*

Start cooking tomatoes, onion and herbs in butter.

7 03   *Drain leeks.*

7 05   *Add leeks to tomato, onion and herbs in saucepan.*

Cover closely and simmer.

Lift out sausages from frying-pan, place in hot dish in bottom of oven, cover.

Oven heat as low as possible.

7 10   *Start frying sliced kidneys and mushrooms.*

7 18   *Lift out kidneys and mushrooms,* put in dish with sausages.

7 20   *Strain tomato sauce through colander.* Pour over sausages, kidneys, etc., and put dish in top of oven, uncovered at low heat.

7 35   *Start cooking potatoes in cold salted water.*

PUT PLATES AND DISHES TO WARM BETWEEN OVEN AND GRILL OR IN RACK COVERED WITH CLOTH

7 40   Crush caramel. Pour syrup over oranges, scatter caramel over.

       Whip and flavour cream, pile on top or put in separate dish.

7 55   (about – test) Drain and dry potatoes. Mash with milk, butter and seasoning. Put in hot dish and cover.

8 0   *Lift out leeks, put in hot dish.* Remove herbs from saucepan and pour contents over leeks.

If people are late, you should cover the dish containing the kidneys, etc., and turn down the oven heat as low as possible.

The mashed potatoes will not come to harm if the vegetable dish containing them is left on the plate-rack with a moderate flame burning underneath.

Put a saucepan containing the leeks by the edge of the stove to keep thoroughly hot, and only take the leeks out at the last moment. Remove the herbs at 8 o'clock or you may forget them.

BRAISED VEAL

POTATOES DUCHESSE

STUFFED PEPPERS

PEACH SURPRISE

RECIPE 1.

Braised Veal. (Cost: about 2/8½.)

1 lb. fillet of English veal	½ oz. flour.
1 lb. mixed carrot, turnip and	1½ ozs. butter
onion	½ pint water (or stock)
1½ ozs. flour	½ lemon

Buy a pound of fillet of English veal. Ask your butcher to cut it fairly thin – about half an inch thick. Trim away skin from the veal and cut it into eight or ten pieces with a sharp knife.

Buy a pound of mixed vegetables – carrot, turnip and onion. It is quite a usual thing to do and the greengrocer will not be surprised. Wash and scrape the carrots and cut them into rings; wash, quarter and peel the turnip; peel and slice the onion. If you happen to have any sticks of celery about, wash them, peel away any stringy parts, cut them up and add them to the other vegetables.

Heat an ounce of butter in a saucepan. When it sizzles loudly, add the pieces of veal and just brown them on both sides. This will take about two minutes. Put the pieces in a casserole, close the lid and keep warm while you proceed to fry the vegetables in the butter until they are all a little browned – about eight minutes. Now lift out the vegetables with a strainer spoon, and put them with the veal in the casserole.

Add a dessertspoonful of flour to the butter remaining in the casserole – if it has all disappeared, add another small piece of butter and heat it till it hisses – and mix well with a large spoon. Take the saucepan to the edge of the stove and add, little by little, rather less than half a pint of hot water (or stock if you have any), blending vigorously all the time with the spoon. You will have to work hard, as the sauce must be perfectly smooth, not a lump anywhere. When quite smooth, return to the fire and bring to the boil, still stirring. Add a tablespoonful of lemon juice, pepper and salt, and simmer for a minute or two, then pour the sauce over the veal and vegetables in the casserole, close the lid tightly, and cook in a moderate oven for about an hour and ten minutes.

Serve in the casserole in which it was cooked.

RECIPE 2.
Potatoes Duchesse. (Cost: about 4d.)

1 lb. potatoes	1 egg
½ oz. butter	Pepper, salt
1 tablespoonful milk	

Wash and peel a pound of potatoes and cook them

in boiling salted water with the lid half off for twenty minutes. Drain the potatoes *well*, return them to the warm saucepan and mash them with a fork very thoroughly, together with half an ounce of butter and a tablespoonful of warm milk. Season with pepper and salt.

Crack an egg against the side of a cup and let the white drip down while you turn the yolk from one half of the shell to the other. Beat the yolk for a minute and add it to the potatoes, stirring them well together. Now put the potato mixture on a floured board and shape with your hands into small rounds or, if you prefer, cut them with a knife into squares, about one inch thick. Mark them with a fork, brush them over with a little of the white of the egg in the cup (using a pastry brush) and put them on a greased baking tin. Do not cover.

Cook in a moderately hot oven for fifteen minutes.

RECIPE 3.
Stuffed Peppers. (Cost: about 5½d.)

½ lb. red peppers	½ lb. tomatoes
1 teaspoonful dried herbs	Breadcrumbs
Pepper, salt	

Buy half a pound of red peppers. (They are sometimes called capsicums in the shops.) Wipe them, cut off the stalk end and remove the core and seeds with a sharp knife.

Dip half a pound of tomatoes into boiling water for a few seconds, take them out, cool them and peel off the skins. Smash up the tomatoes with a wooden spoon until they are pulpy – there is no need to make the mixture perfectly smooth. Add a teaspoonful of mixed dried herbs, salt, pepper and enough breadcrumbs to make the mixture firm. Cram this stuffing, a teaspoonful at a time, into the peppers. Set them on a greased baking tin, uncovered.

Bake in a moderate oven for twenty minutes – if they are longer in the oven, the peppers will shrivel and become tough, so take care.

RECIPE 4.
Peach Surprise. (Cost: about 1/6.)

5 peaches	2 tablespoonfuls red jam
4d. worth cream	2 tablespoonfuls castor sugar
½ lemon	

Every year peaches grow cheaper, and it is possible now to buy five excellent ones for a shilling. Buy a shillingsworth – not the deep orange 'Clingstone' peaches, but the paler ones.

Peel the peaches carefully, cut four of them along the natural line of division, pull them gently in halves with your hands, and take out the stone without damaging the peaches. Put these four peaches into grapefruit glasses. Now whip up four pennyworth of cream until it is stiff, and then add two tablespoonfuls of castor sugar. Do not whip the cream any more after the addition of the sugar. Put a dollop of this sweetened cream between each of the halved peaches, so that it takes the place of a stone.

Mash the fifth peach to a pulp with a wooden spoon, and add to it the juice of half a lemon and four tablespoonfuls from any jar of red jam that you may be using at the moment – raspberry, strawberry cherry or plum. Pour this over sauce the peaches and cream AT THE LAST MOMENT, or it may turn brown.

SHOPPING LIST

			s.	d.
Butcher.				
1 lb. fillet of English veal	...	...	2	4
Dairy.				
Cream		...	0	4
1 egg		...	0	2
Greengrocer.				
1 lb. mixed carrots, onions, turnips ...		...	0	2
1 lb. potatoes		...	0	1½
½ lb. red peppers		...	0	3
¼ lb. tomatoes		...	0	2½
1 lemon		...	0	1
5 peaches		...	1	0
From Stock.				
2 ozs. butter		...	0	2
Sugar, jam		...	0	1
Flour, herbs, breadcrumbs			negligible	
			4	11

TIME-TABLE

DINNER AT EIGHT O'CLOCK

N.B. – If you are dining at a different time, calculate from the time-table at which hour you will have to start your preparations and then alter the hands of the kitchen clock to conform with the time-table. You will find it easier than making individual calculations over every item.

---

6 10 Wash, peel and slice vegetables for veal.
Trim and cut up veal.
6 17 *Heat butter for veal.*
6 18 *Fry veal.*
6 20 *Lift out veal, fry vegetables.*
6 28 *Lift out vegetables, add to veal.*
Light oven.
Start making gravy for veal.
6 40 *Pour gravy over veal and vegetables.*
Put veal in oven.
6 42 Peel potatoes.
6 50 Stuff peppers.

LAY THE TABLE

7 05 *Start boiling potatoes.*
Prepare peaches, whip cream and mix syrup. Do not actually add cream or syrup to peaches until as near serving-time as possible. Set aside in a cool place.
7 25 *Start cooking peppers in oven.*
7 30 *Drain potatoes.*
Warm milk, beat up yolk of egg.
Mash potatoes with milk and egg. Season. Make into cakes.

7 40   Put potatoes in oven.

7 45   PUT PLATES AND DISHES TO WARM IN BOTTOM OF
OVEN.

7 50   *Lower oven heat as much as possible.*
Dish up peppers and potatoes and keep in bottom
of oven.

7 55   Put cream between peaches. Pour jam syrup over
and put on a tray ready to serve.

If people are late the peppers and potatoes had better
remain where they are, covered. The veal is perfectly safe
in its casserole.

JUGGED HARE AND VEGETABLES
RICE

PINEAPPLE CREAM

RECIPE 1.

Jugged Hare. (Cost: about 3/6.)

1 hare	½ lb. jar red currant jelly
1 lb. onions	¼ lb. butter
1 lb. carrots	1 gill wine vinegar
½ lb. turnips	2 ozs. flour
1 lemon	Pepper, salt
Pinch of herbs	1 bay leaf

Buy a Scotch hare. Tell the poulterer to *skin and chop it*, and ask him not to send the blood, unless you have any idea of making a sauce out of it, in which case this recipe is not for you. The pieces of hare will probably be covered with blood. Wash them well, and leave them to soak in cold water until you start cooking. (Put the head and any pieces that are chiefly bone in a saucepan with plenty of cold water, salt, pepper, some parsley and an onion and carrot, peeled. If you bring this to the boil and simmer it for some hours, adding any spare bits of vegetable you come across, you will make good hare soup next day.)

Peel and slice a pound of onions. Wash and scrape a pound of carrots and cut them into rings about as thick as a florin. Wash half a pound of turnips, quarter them, peel them, and if still very large cut into eighths. Squeeze out the juice of a lemon and strain it. Tie up a pinch of herbs in muslin. Put two tablespoonfuls of sieved flour on a plate with a tea-spoonful of salt and a good pinch of pepper and mix together.

When all these preliminaries are over, heat two ounces of butter in a *large* saucepan. Dry the pieces of hare in a cloth, roll them in the seasoned flour, and when the butter is very hot, fry them in it quickly for five or six minutes, turning them so that they brown but do not burn.

Now lift out the pieces of hare, add two ounces of butter to that already in the pan, and fry all the vegetables in the butter for seven or eight minutes. Then return the hare to the saucepan with the vege-tables and add half a small cupful of wine vinegar together with the lemon juice, dried herbs tied in muslin and a bay leaf. Season with plenty of pepper and salt. Cover the saucepan closely, pressing down the lid over a piece of greaseproof paper and simmer at a very low heat for two hours.

Half an hour before serving, add a full dessert-spoonful of red currant jelly from the half-pound jar which you will serve up with the hare.

To dish up, remove the herbs and bay leaf and throw them away. Lift out the vegetables with a strainer spoon, and pile them at either end of a large dish. Lift out the pieces of hare and place in the centre. Sprinkle a dessertspoonful of flour into the liquid left at the bottom of the saucepan and go on cooking it for a few minutes, stirring vigorously and squashing away any lumps that may try to form. Either pour this gravy over the hare or serve it separately, whichever you prefer. (If you happen to have any sour cream in the house, add it to the sauce and stir well.)

Don't forget the red currant jelly.

RECIPE 2.

Plain Boiled Rice. (Cost: about 2d.)

    ½lb. rice   Water   Salt

Allow one small cupful of rice to two people. Wash it either by putting it in a gravy strainer and running cold water through or by putting the rice in a large bowl and running in cold water. The rice will sink and the dirt will rise in the water and flow away; do this several times.

Throw the rice into PLENTY of boiling salted water. Let it boil fast, but not 'gallop', and stir from time to time so that the rice circulates evenly and does not stick to the sides or bottom of the pan. After fifteen minutes it should be cooked, or very nearly. Test it by rubbing a grain between your finger and thumb. If it just rubs away, it is cooked.

Turn out the rice into the colander, and run cold water from the tap through it – don't keep on doing this till the rice is cold. Drain thoroughly. The rice should not be a slimy mass – every grain should be distinct and firm. Dry the saucepan.

As soon as the rice is drained, return it to the saucepan, and set it at the edge of the stove with a dry cloth folded over the top of the saucepan to keep the rice warm and absorb any moisture that might turn it soggy.

Serve the rice either separately or in little piles round the dish of hare.

RECIPE 3.
Pineapple Cream. (Cost: about 1/2½.)

1 small tin pineapple	6d. worth cream
4 small sheets of gelatine	Some chopped pistachio
1 gill milk	nuts
	2 ozs. castor sugar

Put four small sheets of gelatine (about thre inches by nine inches) into one small cupful of milk in a saucepan and heat slowly, stirring until the gelatine is dissolved. Strain into a large bowl. Turn out the contents of a small tin of pineapple (cubes or slices) and cut the pieces of pineapple up small. Add them, together with the juice, to the milk and gelatine, mix well and add two tablespoonfuls of sugar, let all stand until partly set (i.e., until it is just beginning to turn solid). This will take different lengths of time according to the weather and the

213

temperature of the kitchen. Watch carefully in winter, when it sets very quickly.

Meanwhile, whip sixpennyworth of cream stiffly. As soon as the pineapple is partly set, add the cream and beat all together for a minute. Pour into a wet mould to finish setting.

Turn out, when set, on to the dish in which you mean to serve it. This sweet, though extremely good, sometimes looks a dull greyish white and if this should happen its appearance will be much improved by scattering some finely-chopped pistachio nuts (which you can buy by the ounce from grocers and some confectioners) over the top. Another way of colouring it is to add a few drops of liquid colouring (also bought from the grocer) when you mix the milk and pineapple.

N.B. – Don't be snobbish about the pineapple. The smallest and cheapest tin will do. Try using other fruit in the same way.

SEVEN DINNERS FOR AUTUMN

SHOPPING LIST

Poulterer.						s.	d.
A Scotch hare, skinned and chopped ...			...		...	2	3
Dairy.							
Cream ...	...	...	...	...	...	0	6
¼ lb. butter	...	...	...	...	...	0	3
Greengrocer.							
1 lb. onions	...	...	...	...	...	0	1½
1 lb. carrots	...	...	...	...	...	0	1½
½ lb. turnips	...	...	...	...	...	0	1
1 lemon	...	...	...	...	...	0	1
Grocer.							
½ lb. jar red currant jelly		...	...	...	0	5
½ lb. rice	...	...	...	...	...	0	2
1 small tin pineapple ...		...	...	...	0	5½
From Stock.							
Vinegar (1 gill) ...	...	...	...	...	0	2
1 gill milk	...	...	...	...	...	0	1
4 sheets gelatine	...	...	...	...	0	1
Pistachio nuts ...	...	...	...	...	0	1
Flour, herbs, bay leaf, sugar	...	...	...	0	0½

4 11

TIME-TABLE

DINNER AT EIGHT O'CLOCK

N.B. – If you are dining at a different time, calculate
from the time-table the hour at which you will have to

start your preparations and then alter the hands of the kitchen clock to conform with the time-table. You will find it easier than making individual calculations.

You will have to prepare this dinner early because of the hare, which must start cooking by six o'clock. Once the hare is simmering, you can cook the sweet in three-quarters of an hour and leave it for over an hour to set – but if your kitchen is a very hot one, you had better put your mind at rest by making the sweet during the morning or on the previous evening.

Leave yourself plenty of time at the beginning to prepare the hare and vegetables.

5 0   Peel and slice onions.
Wash and scrape carrots and cut in rings.
Wash, quarter and peel turnips.
Squeeze out lemon juice.
Tie up pinch of herbs in muslin.
Prepare seasoned flour.
Wash and dry hare and roll in seasoned flour.

5 45   *Start heating butter in large saucepan.*

5 47   *Start frying pieces of hare.*

5 52   *Lift out pieces of hare,* keep warm. *Add butter to saucepan.*
Start frying vegetables.

6 0   *Return pieces of hare to saucepan with vegetables.* Add lemon juice, vinegar, herbs, bay leaf, salt and pepper. *Cover saucepan tightly and simmer.*

ALL YOU HAVE TO REMEMBER ABOUT THE HARE NOW IS TO ADD A DESSERTSPOONFUL OF RED CURRANT JELLY AT 7.30

START ON THE SWEET

6 02   Heat milk and gelatine, stirring.

6 06   (about) Strain milk and gelatine into large bowl. Turn out tin of pineapple, chop up fruit.

6 10   Mix pineapple, sugar and juice with milk and gelatine, leave to set.

Whip up cream.

6 45   (about) (possibly earlier) Add whipped cream to partly-set pineapple and milk, beat all well together for a minute, put in a wet mould in a cool place to finish setting.

NOW YOU HAVE ONLY THE RICE TO COOK, AND AN INTERVAL OF FORTY MINUTES

7 25   *Start boiling salted water for rice.*

Wash rice.

7 30   *Add red currant jelly to hare.*

LAY THE TABLE

7 40   *Start boiling rice.*

PUT PLATES AND DISHES TO WARM IN RACK

Turn out sweet and decorate with pistachio nuts.

7 55   *Run cold water into rice, drain.* Dry saucepan, return rice to saucepan and set at edge of stove with dry cloth folded over.

7 58   Lift out hare and vegetables, place on hot dish, keep warm. Add dessertspoonful of flour to liquid in pan, simmer and stir thoroughly.

The flour should boil for at least five minutes in the gravy, but it is as well not to start on this until you are sure that your guests have arrived. A few minutes earlier or later will not make much difference to them, but a lot of difference to the hare, which can go on simmering without harm for an indefinite time, but, once it has been put on a plate, will get cold or dry.

FILLETS OF WHITING
(WITH SPAGHETTI MILANAISE)

GERMAN CHOCOLATE PUDDING

There is really no special reason why this menu should be an autumn one. It would be equally good at any season of the year, and cheapest in spring, when the price of eggs (used in the pudding) is at its lowest. The fish course is comparatively cheap, and so allows you to spend rather more money than usual on the sweet, which is one of the most delicious we know.

RECIPE 1.
Fillets of Whiting. (Cost: about 2/6.)

2½ lbs. fresh whiting (filleted)	½ lb. spaghetti
1 gill milk	2 tomatoes
1 bay leaf	2 onions
2 ozs. butter	Pinch of herbs
1 lemon	1 tablespoonful grated
2 ozs. flour	Parmesan cheese
Pepper, salt	

Buy one large fresh whiting, weighing two and a half pounds, or two smaller ones. Ask the fishmonger to fillet them and implore him to take ALL the skin off – fishmongers, unless specially pleaded with, have a deplorable way of sending fillets of fish with skin on one side. You can skin the fish yourself at home with a sharp knife, but it is a wearisome and quite unnecessary extra job. If the whiting is a very large one, ask the fishmonger to cut each fillet in two.

Mix a dessertspoonful of salt with a quarter of a teaspoonful of pepper on a plate. Rub each fillet on both sides with the mixture. Put a bay leaf in the bottom of a flat fireproof dish. Lay the seasoned fillets flat in the dish, sprinkle them with the juice of half a lemon (or, if you have any, a tablespoonful of sherry) and pour round them a teacupful of warm milk. Put a few little dabs of butter on top of the fillets. Cover with a piece of greased paper.

Cook in a moderate oven for thirty minutes. Test the fillets with a knitting-needle. They should be soft, but not falling to pieces.

While the whiting is cooking in the oven you must prepare the spaghetti milanaise to go with it.

Spaghetti Milanaise. Peel and chop two onions. Wipe two really ripe tomatoes and cut them in quarters. Put the tomatoes in a saucepan with half an ounce of butter, the chopped onions, a pinch of herbs tied up in muslin, a teaspoonful of salt and half a teaspoonful of pepper. In about eight or ten minutes the tomatoes will be cooked; strain the *purée* through the colander into a bowl. Keep this warm while you start on the spaghetti itself.

Break the spaghetti into pieces of about the length of your middle finger and throw them into plenty of boiling salted water. Let them cook fast for about fifteen minutes. Test, by lifting out a piece – it will be very hot – the spaghetti should be soft, but of a 'tacky' consistency, and not sodden. While it is cooking you will just have time to complete the *milanaise sauce*.

Melt an ounce of butter in the saucepan in which you cooked the tomatoes and onion. When it is melted and very hot, add a tablespoonful of flour and blend thoroughly into the butter with a wooden spoon. Take the saucepan to the edge of the stove and add gradually, stirring all the time, the strained tomato *purée*. If, when all is added, the mixture is still very solid, you must then add a little warm water and thin it out, still stirring. It should be like very thick cream in consistency and coloured red. Now return the saucepan to the flame, bring the sauce to the boil, still stirring, and let it boil gently all over for a few minutes. Set the saucepan at the edge of the stove while you drain the spaghetti thoroughly (unless it was cooked first and had already been well drained and put in a warm bowl).

Finally, pour the sauce over the spaghetti and mix the two gently, but thoroughly, so that the spaghetti is completely coated and of a delicate red colour.

To serve the whiting, lift the fillets carefully from the milk with a fish-slice and pile them in the middle of a large hot dish. Arrange the spaghetti round the fillets or at either end of the dish, and sprinkle it with about a tablespoonful of finely grated cheese.

RECIPE 2.

German Chocolate Pudding. (Cost: about 2/4.)

½ lb. bitter chocolate	¾ pint milk (3 gills)
A 6d. sponge cake or 6 penny sponge cakes	2 eggs
	About 2½ ozs. white sugar
4d. worth cream	Few drops vanilla (or ½-inch stick)
Chocolate hailstones	

Take a half-pound block of hard, unsweetened chocolate, break it into small pieces and melt it in a saucepan with about a teacupful of milk and a little castor sugar to taste.

Cut a sixpenny block of sponge cake (it should not be very stale) or six oblong sponge cakes into very thin slices, so thin that you can almost see through them. Put a layer of the hot chocolate in a glass dish, then a layer of the sponge slices and continue until you have used up your ingredients. The last layer should be one of chocolate. Let it all get very cold.

Now make a *custard*. Break two eggs into the top of a double boiler and add two tablespoonfuls of castor sugar. Beat slightly. Heat half a pint of milk with a few drops of vanilla essence (or half an inch of vanilla pod) in a double-lipped saucepan until the milk is nearly boiling. Put hot water in the bottom half of the double boiler, and put over it the top half of the boiler with the eggs in it and pour the hot milk over the eggs, stirring all the time with a wooden spoon. Continue to heat the double boiler gently and to stir the custard in the top section until you can feel the custard beginning to thicken under the spoon. Then take the boiler away from the stove, and go on for a minute until you are satisfied with the thickness of the custard, and sure that it is quite smooth. Stir in fourpennyworth of cream and pour the hot custard over the top layer of chocolate in the dish – the chocolate should be absolutely cold, remember. Let the custard, too, get very cold (in the ice-box or refrigerator, if you possess one – extreme cold improves this dish enormously). Decorate at the last moment with chocolate hailstones, which you can buy from good grocers by the pound, or less, and store in a tin.

SEVEN DINNERS FOR AUTUMN

SHOPPING LIST

		s.	d.
Fishmonger.			
2½ lbs. fresh whiting, skinned and filleted ...		1	8
(Fillets to be cut in halves if very large)			
Dairy.			
2 eggs		0	4
1 pint milk (1 gill for fish, 1 for chocolate, ½ pint			
for custard)		0	3
Cream		0	4
Baker.			
1 block of sponge cake, or 6 small sponge cakes ...		0	6
Greengrocer.			
1 lemon		0	1
Grocer.			
¼ lb. Italian spaghetti		0	2
½ lb. unsweetened chocolate		0	10½
From Stock.			
2 tomatoes, 2 onions		0	2½
1 tablespoonful grated Parmesan cheese ...		0	2
Chocolate hailstones		0	0½
4 ozs. sugar		0	1
Flour, bay leaf, herbs, vanilla, individually neg-			
ligible, but at most		0	1
		4	**9½**

TIME-TABLE

DINNER AT EIGHT O'CLOCK

N.B. – If you are dining at a different time, calculate from the time-table the hour at which you will have to start your preparations and then alter the hands of the kitchen clock to conform with the time-table. You will find this easier than making calculations over the individual items.

———

Make the chocolate pudding early so that it may get very cold. It will not take more than half an hour to do the actual cooking, but you must allow intervals for cooling. Allow at least an hour for the final cooling, and stand the dish in some cold and draughty spot (if you have one) or in a basin of very cold water.

6 0   Make sweet.   WASH UP

6 50   LAY THE TABLE

7 0   Peel and chop onions.
      Wipe and quarter tomatoes.
      Squeeze lemon juice.
      Tie herbs up in muslin.
      Break up spaghetti.

7 20   *Light the oven.*
      Start cooking tomatoes with onion, etc., for sauce for spaghetti.
      Prepare fillets for cooking.

7 30   *Start cooking fish in moderate oven.*
      Start boiling salted water for spaghetti.

PUT PLATES AND BOWL TO WARM BETWEEN OVEN AND GRILL OR ON PLATE-RACK COVERED WITH CLOTH

7 35   *Strain tomato purée.* Keep warm.

7 40   *Start boiling spaghetti.*
      Start making sauce for spaghetti.

7 55   *Put sauce by edge of stove to keep warm.*
      Drain spaghetti, put in warm bowl, pour sauce over and mix well. Keep warm.

8   o   Turn out oven. Lift out fillets of fish and pile on hot dish. Arrange spaghetti round or at each end. Decorate sweet with chocolate hailstones.

If people are late, you should turn down the oven as low as possible, leave the fillets in the milk and cover them. Cover the bowl containing the flavoured spaghetti and stand it in a frying-pan of gently-boiling water.

CHAPTER VI

Winter Menu No. 1   FOR FOUR PEOPLE

SPICED BEEF AND BUTTER BEANS

ARTICHOKES AND TOMATOES

ANGELS' CREAM

RECIPE 1.

Spiced Beef and Butter Beans. (Cost: about 3/1.)

4 lbs. unsalted brisket (English)	2 ozs. brown sugar
or 3 lbs. chilled topside	1 teaspoonful ground
1 lb. butter beans (dried)	ginger
1 onion	6 cloves
1 gill water	¼ teaspoonful mace
	Pepper, salt

SOAK a pound of dried butter beans in a large bowl with plenty of water for twelve hours. Then skin them.

Buy four pounds of fresh brisket or three pounds of chilled topside. Tell the butcher that you want the brisket as lean as possible – it is a very fat cut of meat – and ask him to roll it for you. (He will give you the bones separately, and you can make soup next day by simmering these with vegetables and any beans that are left over.)

Chop a medium-sized onion. Put the beef in a large saucepan and add the chopped onion, the

226

beans (drained), two tablespoonfuls of brown sugar, a teaspoonful of ground ginger, six cloves, a quarter of a teaspoonful of mace, half a breakfastcupful of water, pepper and salt.

Close the lid of the saucepan tightly over a piece of greaseproof paper and simmer over a *very* low heat for four hours. After three and a half hours you must take off the lid and skim off as much fat as possible. If you like the gravy with your meat to be thick rather than thin, sprinkle in a tablespoonful of sieved flour at the same time. Replace the lid.

To serve, lift out the meat and carve it in slices, and put them overlapping on a hot dish in a warm place. The beef should be quite soft, almost crumbling, in fact, and a dark brown colour. Lift out the beans with a strainer spoon and pile them at either end of the dish. Pick out the cloves and throw them away. Raise the heat below the saucepan for a minute or two while you give the liquid left in the saucepan a good stirring. You can either pour it over the beans or serve it separately.

RECIPE 2.
Artichokes and Tomatoes. (Cost: about 7d.)
 2 lbs. Jerusalem artichokes
 1 small tin peeled tomatoes
 Salt, pepper

Wash and peel two pounds of Jerusalem artichokes. If they have awkward, nobbly shapes, cut them into simpler ones before peeling them. It will be easier and will waste less artichoke. Artichoke skin is as tough as the bark of a tree, so see that every bit of it is pared away.

Parboil the artichokes by cooking them in plenty of boiling salted water for about fifteen minutes. Lift them out and drain. Put the peeled artichokes into a fireproof dish with the contents of the tomato tin, add pepper and salt, but no water. Close the lid and cook in the oven at a fairly low heat for an hour and a half. The tomatoes will supply the artichokes with enough liquid to cook in.

Serve in the dish in which they were cooked.

(NOTE: This recipe can be made into the basis of a delicious and economical stew, which has another advantage in that it can be left to cook itself. Cut up some fresh stewing steak, or the meaty parts of some mutton, or cold meat left on a joint into small pieces. Put them, with plenty of seasoning, into a fireproof dish with the parboiled artichokes and tinned tomatoes, cover and cook at *very* low heat for four hours.)

RECIPE 3.

Angels' Cream. (Cost: about 1/2.)

5 bananas	3 ozs. brown sugar
2 oranges	2d. worth cream
1 lemon	4 sheets gelatine
12 almonds	¾ gill water

This is a cold sweet made from bananas flavoured with orange and lemon and eaten with a sauce of orange, cream and almonds. Naturally, if you want to, you will soon think of ways of varying the sauce or enriching the consistency of the sweet – which might, by the way, be made equally well with other fruits, e.g., prunes or peaches.

Peel five bananas, which must have no black, over-ripe portions on them, and mash them with a fork in a basin. Add a tablespoonful of brown sugar and the juice of a lemon and an orange. Mix all together.

Heat a quarter of a teacupful of water in a sauce-pan. When the water is warm, add four small sheets of gelatine (about three inches by nine inches) and stir very thoroughly until the gelatine is dissolved. Strain this, and add it to the bananas, and beat all well together. Pour into separate glasses which you have rinsed out in cold water, and leave to set in a cool place. The time for setting varies, but on an ordinary day, neither very hot nor very cold, it will be just under an hour.

Make the sauce while the banana is setting. Squeeze out the juice of an orange and cut a dozen or so very thin slices from the outside skin (which you have wiped carefully). Heat two tablespoonfuls of brown sugar in half a teacupful of water in a sauce-pan, stirring. When it boils, add the orange juice and slices of peel and simmer for about ten minutes, stir-ring from time to time. Meanwhile drop about a dozen almonds into boiling water and leave them there for a minute. Then run some cold water into the pan, slip the almonds out of their skins with your fingers and put them into a cup of cold water with a few drops of vinegar to keep them white.

When the orange syrup has simmered for ten minutes, strain it into a cup and leave it to cool.

A few minutes before you want to serve the sweet, dry the almonds and chop them coarsely. Stir a little cream (twopennyworth will do) into the orange syrup which will then turn a biscuit colour. Pour a little of this thin sauce into each glass of banana cream and scatter some chopped almonds on top.

SHOPPING LIST

		s.	d.
Butcher.			
4 lbs. fresh brisket (English) boned and rolled or 3 lbs. chilled topside		2	8
Dairy.			
Cream		0	2
Greengrocer.			
2 lbs. Jerusalem artichokes		0	3
5 bananas		0	6
2 oranges (small)		0	3
1 lemon		0	1
Grocer.			
1 lb. dried butter beans		0	4
1 tin peeled tomatoes		0	4
From Stock.			
1 onion		0	0½
6 ozs. brown sugar (beef and sweet)		0	1
Gelatine		0	1
Almonds		0	0½
Ginger, cloves, mace – almost negligible, but at most		0	0½
		4	10½

SEVEN DINNERS FOR WINTER

TIME-TABLE

Dinner at Eight O'Clock

N.B. – If you are dining at a different time, calculate from the time-table the hour at which you will have to start your preparations and then alter the hands of the kitchen clock to conform with the time-table. You will find this easier than calculating individual items.

This is an extremely easy dinner to prepare. The beef takes a long time to cook, but it uses very little heat and needs hardly any watching. As for the artichokes, they practically cook themselves. You can either put the beef on to cook at four o'clock or, if this is impossible, give it a preliminary two hours' simmering in the morning or during the previous evening. Supposing it has already simmered for two hours and been allowed to get cold, you should start to cook it again at a little before six o'clock, so that it may have a little extra time in which to heat through. The sweet takes about half an hour to cook, and an hour to cool. The beans take fifteen minutes to skin.

Let us assume that the beef has been cooked for two hours.

5 45   *Start cooking beef at low heat.*
      Start boiling salted water for artichokes.
      Wash and peel artichokes.

6 0   *Start cooking artichokes.*
      Light oven.

Lay the Table

6 15   Turn out tomatoes, with liquid, into fireproof dish.
      Drain artichokes, add to tomatoes, season, close lid and *start cooking in oven.*
      Start making sweet and sauce for sweet.

231

6 45   Put sweet to set and sauce to cool.

YOU HAVE NOW NOTHING TO DO BUT WASH UP UNTIL 7 30

7 30   Skim fat off beef, sprinkle in flour if desired.

PUT PLATES AND DISHES TO WARM BETWEEN OVEN AND GRILL

7 50   Dry and chop almonds.
           Add cream to orange syrup, stir and pour over banana cream.
           Sprinkle chopped almonds over syrup.

7 55   Lift out beef and beans, place on hot dish and carve.
           Finish cooking gravy in saucepan. Stir, pour over beans or dish up separately.

If people are late, turn down the oven heat as low as possible and leave the artichokes and tomatoes where they are. Leave the beef and beans to continue simmering in the saucepan. Nothing will be hurt.

STEAK AND KIDNEY PIE

BRAISED ONIONS

CREAMED POTATOES

HOT FRUIT COMPOTE

The whole of this meal goes into the oven two hours before dinner, leaving you with practically nothing more to do until you serve it up. It can be quite easily kept back if people are late.

RECIPE I.
Steak and Kidney Pie. (Cost: about 3/-.)

1½ lbs. stewing steak	10 ozs. flour (8 ozs. for
¼ lb. ox kidney	pastry)
A little potato, if needed,	6 ozs. butter
to fill pie-dish	1 egg
Pepper, salt	A little lemon juice
½ teaspoonful baking powder	

Buy a pound and a half of lean stewing steak and a quarter of a pound of ox kidney. Cut the steak into neat pieces, trimming away every bit of skin, gristle and fat, however small, and putting these discards into a saucepan with pepper and salt and enough cold water to cover them well. Remove core and skin from the kidney and cut it into pieces; add the core and any piece of kidney sticking to it to the oddments of steak in the saucepan. The success of a steak and kidney pie largely depends on ALL the meat inside it being tender and well-flavoured, so pay strict attention to this initial trimming.

Sift two tablespoonfuls of flour with a teaspoonful of salt and half a teaspoonful of pepper on to a plate. Roll each piece of steak and kidney in the seasoned flour and then place it in the pie-dish. The meat will be enough for four people, but may not fill your pie-dish if it is a large one. If it does not fill the dish, then turn it out and put a layer of raw sliced potato at the bottom and the meat above. The potato tastes good, colours dark brown during cooking and fills up the dish to the brim – which is essential to give support to the crust.

Add two tablespoonfuls of water – no more. Put an inverted egg-cup or a pie-crust prop in the centre of the dish.

To make the pie-crust.

Sieve half a pound of flour with a pinch of salt and half a teaspoonful of baking powder into a LARGE bowl. (It is fatal to try and mix pastry in a basin only just large enough to hold the ingredients.) Put six ounces of butter into the flour and cut it up into pieces with a knife. Then rub the butter lightly and quickly into the flour with the tips of the fingers, lifting the flour as you do so, until the mixture resembles fine breadcrumbs.

Separate the yolk from the white of an egg by

cracking the egg against the side of a basin and letting the white drip down while you turn the yolk from one half of the shell to the other until it is free of white. Squeeze out the juice of a lemon, strain it and whip up the yolk slightly with a teaspoonful of the lemon juice.

Make a little hole in the middle of the flour mixture and turn in the yolk; mix it in quickly with a pastry-knife. Add a dessertspoonful of cold water and mix again. Now knead the mixture with the knuckles of your hands until it forms a ball of dough, free from cracks, and leaves the sides of the basin quite clean. Don't leave any bits unaccounted for in the basin, but weld the whole together very thoroughly. Turn out on to a lightly-floured board and knead again a little. Turn the dough round and round with one hand while you gently press cracks together with the fingertips of the other.

Flour your rolling-pin and roll out lightly and quickly in one direction – always *away* from ,you – until you have a piece of pastry of the same shape as your pie-dish, but about an inch larger all round. (This amount of pastry will make a cover for a dish measuring about nine inches by six.) The crust should be about a quarter of an inch thick. Cut off round the edge a half-inch wide strip, long enough to go round the rim of the pastry-dish – or, if this is difficult, several shorter strips, each half an inch wide. (Be very careful that you do not reduce the main part of your pastry to a size smaller than that of the dish.) Now moisten the rim of your pie-dish with water and lay the strips of pastry along it; moisten any edges where they meet, as this will join them together in the cooking. Next, lift the main pastry lid very carefully with the help of your pastry-knife and fit it over the pie-dish. It is very important indeed not to stretch this lid; let it sink into place easily and not be drawn taut anywhere. Mark the edges with a knife or fork, pressing down the edge of the pastry upon the foundation layer strip which you put round the rim of the dish.

You can now make decorations for the middle of the pie by gathering up the scraps of pastry on the board and rolling them into a strip about one and a half inches wide. Mark this with slanting lines about two inches apart and cut along these, making diamond-shaped pieces. Mark each diamond of pastry with the back of a knife to imitate veins and you will have the good old traditional 'leaves' of pastry.

If you aspire to a 'rose', then roll out a thin piece of pastry, cut it into a square and fold this in four as you would a letter going into an envelope. Cut across the centre of this smaller square, going right through, but just not quite to the edges. Put this cut square over the tip of your first finger and open up the edges of the cross, which will then look like formal petals. It is difficult to make this operation perfectly clear in words, but if you experiment a little you will at least make something as a centre-piece for your pie, whether it is a triumph of confectionery or not.

236

Plunge your knife straight down through the pastry beside the centre support to allow a vent for steam. If you want to glaze your pie on top, brush it over now with water or beaten egg – if you use yolk only, you will get a deeper glaze.

Put the pie in a hot oven and cook it quickly for about half an hour – the pastry will then be cooked, but not the meat inside the pie, so put the pie in a cooler, but not COOL part of the oven for another hour and a half to finish cooking. If, before the end of this time, the pastry begins to get too brown (it should be a golden yellow or very, very pale brown) cover over the pie with some greaseproof paper.

While the pie is cooking you must set your saucepan of discards to simmer very, very gently on the top of the oven. If you have any odd vegetables or green top of celery, add this to the rest. Leave the lid of the pan half on. The stock obtained in this way will be infinitely better than hot water for making gravy inside the pie. About twenty minutes before the latter is due to be cooked, strain your stock, squashing its contents against the bottom of a sieve or strainer, and very, very carefully pour the stock (using a funnel if you have one) through the vent in the crust into the pie.

If you use an egg-cup to support your crust, remember that gravy is likely to accumulate underneath it and lift it slightly as soon as you cut the pie to release the hidden store of gravy.

RECIPE 2.

Braised Onions. (Cost: about 5d.)

> 4 large onions, or 8 smaller ones
> 2 ozs. butter
> Salt, pepper

Remember that onions, when cooked whole, take longer than any other vegetables, except the 'root' tribe – parsnip, turnip, beet, swede and carrot. This dish will be spoilt unless the onions are cooked absolutely soft.

Choose four large onions of even size – or eight smaller ones. Peel them and put them in boiling salted water; boil, with the lid half on, for forty-five minutes. Now drain the onions and put them in a fireproof dish with a good piece of butter and a sprinkling of pepper and salt on the top of each. Cover with greaseproof paper – it is best to allow each onion its own cap of paper – and cook in a moderate oven for two hours. When finished, the onions should be meltingly soft, but still whole, and slightly browned. Serve them in the dish in which they were cooked.

RECIPE 3.
Creamed Potatoes. (Cost: about 4½d.)

1½ lbs. potatoes	Pepper, salt
½ oz. butter	½ pint milk

Peel the potatoes and cut them into slices about a quarter of an inch thick. Dry these in a cloth and put them in layers in a fireproof dish. Sprinkle each layer with pepper and salt. Pour in the milk and dot the top of the potatoes with small pieces of butter. Cover the dish and cook in the oven for two hours at moderate heat.

When you are ready to serve this dish, take a fork and lightly mash the potatoes in with the milk and butter. Serve in the dish in which they were cooked.

RECIPE 4.

Hot Fruit Compote. (Cost: about 1/1½.)

1 small tin pineapple	1 orange
½ lb. cooking pears	1 lemon
1 lb. apples (cooking)	4 ozs. sugar

Open the tin of pineapple, strain the juice into a saucepan and chop the fruit finely. Peel, core and slice the apples and put them into a bowl with the chopped pineapple. Peel the orange, cutting away the white pith as well as the outer skin; do this over the vessel containing the apples, etc., so as not to lose any of the juice. Now take the peeled orange in the left hand and cut with a sharp knife down to the centre, dividing the fruit from one of the skins that mark off the orange into sections; open it out slightly, flick out the pips and turn out the section of orange into the vessel below. Repeat this operation until you have cut out all the fruity part of the orange. This is the neatest way of cutting an orange into sections – though in this particular case it does not matter if the fruit is a bit pulpy and smashed.

Squeeze the remains of the orange left in your hand to extract the last drops of juice.

Add the strained juice of a lemon and four table-spoonfuls of brown sugar to the pineapple juice in the saucepan. (You can use just a teaspoonful of this lemon juice for making the pastry-crust for your meat pie.) Heat, stirring with a wooden spoon, until the juice boils. Then turn in the pineapple, apple and orange and simmer slowly until they are pulpy – about fifteen or twenty minutes.

Now peel, halve and core the pears – do not break them if you can help it. Put the halves in a fireproof dish and cover them with the contents of the sauce-pan. Do not cover the dish. Bake in as slow an oven as possible for three hours.

If your oven is a small one, you may find it difficult to cook the compote at the same time as the rest of the dinner. In this case you must cook it beforehand and eat it cold or else reheat it over a pan of boiling water for half an hour before dinner-time. If, however, you have room to cook it together with the pie and vegetables, put it as near the bottom of the oven as possible, as it ought to be cooked very slowly.

If you succeed in cooking the compote long and slowly it will turn a golden brown and be rather 'toffeeish' round the edges. If circumstances force you to cook it more quickly, do not be sad, for it will not be ruined. Make sure of one thing, however, or failure is certain. The pears MUST be soft.

SEVEN DINNERS FOR WINTER

SHOPPING LIST

		s.	d.
Butcher.			
1½ lbs. stewing steak		1	11
¼ lb. ox kidney		0	4
Dairy.			
1 egg (yolk only required)		0	2
½ lb. butter (for pastry and onions)		0	6
½ pint milk		0	1¾
Greengrocer.			
2 lbs. onions		0	3
1½ lbs. potatoes		0	2½
½ lb. pears		0	2
1 lb. apples		0	3
1 lemon		0	1½
1 orange		0	1½
Grocer.			
1 small tin pineapple		0	4½
From Stock.			
10 ozs. flour		0	1½
½ oz. butter (for potatoes)		0	0½
4 ozs. brown sugar		0	1
		4	9¾

Baking powder, negligible

TIME-TABLE

Dinner at Eight O'Clock

N.B. – If you are dining at a different time, calculate
from the time-table the hour at which you will have to

DINNERS FOR BEGINNERS

start your preparations and then alter the hands of the kitchen clock to conform with the time-table. You will find this easier than making individual calculations over every item.

————

You must begin this dinner rather early, but it has the advantage, as we said before, of leaving you practically free for the last two hours before dinner.

If your oven is too small to take the compote with the pie and the vegetables, then cook the sweet in the morning and heat it up for half an hour before dinner by putting it over a saucepan of boiling water – unless you prefer to eat it cold. Here it is included in the time-table with the rest of the meal.

4 30   Make fruit compote. You can have it in the oven in half an hour.
4 45   *Light the oven.*
5 0   *Put fruit compote in oven at very low heat.*
       Peel onions.
5 05   *Start boiling salted water for onions.*
       Peel, slice and prepare potatoes with milk and butter.
5 15   *Start boiling onions.*

LAY THE TABLE

5 25   Start trimming and preparing meat for pie.
       Put trimmings with water and seasoning to simmer.
5 45   *Increase oven heat for steak and kidney pie. Remove compote to coolest part of oven.*
       Make pie crust.
6 0   *Put pie in oven.*
       Start cooking potatoes in oven.
       Drain onions, season, add butter, cover and start cooking in oven.

242

6 30   *If pastry is golden brown, lower heat in oven.*
          YOU HAVE NOTHING TO DO NOW UNTIL 7 40

7 40   *Strain stock, pour through funnel into pie.*

7 45   Put plates and dishes to warm on top of oven between oven and grill, changing them about so that all get the warmth of the oven roof.

7 50   If the plates are not sufficiently hot, light a ring on the top of the stove and put them in the rack, covered with a cloth.
          Mash potatoes in dish.

If people are late, everything can be kept hot in the oven by reducing the heat as far as possible. See that the pie is covered.

ROASTED STUFFED LOIN OF MUTTON
ROAST POTATOES
CREAMED TURNIPS

CRANBERRY AND APPLE SNOW

RECIPE I.

Roast Stuffed Loin of Mutton and Roast Potatoes. (Cost: about 3/0½.)

2½ lbs. New Zealand loin of mutton	1 egg
1 teacupful breadcrumbs	Dripping
1 oz. suet	Pepper, salt
½ bunch parsley	1 lb. potatoes
Pinch of dried herbs	

Buy two and a half pounds of New Zealand loin of mutton. Ask the butcher to send it boned and ready for rolling – not rolled – and beg him to send with it just an ounce of chopped suet. If he will not chop the suet in such a small quantity, and you do not want the bother of chopping the suet which accompanies the loin, then you must make your stuffing without it.

Crumble some slices of bread until you have a small cupful of crumbs.   Wash and dry half a bunch of parsley and pick the leaves from the stalks. Peel and slice a small onion and chop it and the parsley together. Mix with the breadcrumbs and suet in a basin. Add a sprinkling of pepper, half a

244

teaspoonful of salt and a small pinch of dried herbs. Crack an egg against a cup and let the white drip down into the cup, turn the yolk from one half of the shell to the other until it is free of white. Set the white aside and add the yolk to the stuffing; mix well. The stuffing should form a stiff paste. If it is too dry you must add a very little water.

Wipe the meat and rub it all over with some pepper and salt which you have mixed on a plate in the proportion of a tablespoonful of salt to half a teaspoonful of pepper. Spread the stuffing over the inside of the meat; do not allow the stuffing to come right to the edges, or it will ooze out during the cooking. Roll up the mutton and skewer it neatly together or tie it in two or three places with string.

Make the oven very hot. Put the stuffed mutton in a roasting-pan (without the lid) spread plenty of dripping on top of the meat and roast it in the oven for an hour. Keep the heat very high for the first fifteen minutes; after this, though it should still be high, it need not be so fierce as at first. (The intense heat at the beginning will close the meat and keep it juicy and tender inside.) Turn the mutton once or twice during the first fifteen minutes, and baste it with a long spoon. (Basting means taking up the hot fat with a spoon and pouring it over the object which is being roasted.)

Peel a pound of potatoes and cut them into fairly equal sizes. Dry them. Place them beside or under the meat in the roasting-pan after the first fifteen minutes, and let them go on cooking with the meat until it is finished, when they should be brown and crisp outside, but soft all through within. Turn the potatoes occasionally and baste them with the dripping.

When the meat is cooked, you must take it out and put it on a large hot dish. Drain the potatoes of fat and put them either round the meat or in a separate hot dish. Turn the oven heat down as low as possible and put the dish with the meat and potatoes back in the oven while you make the gravy to go with it.
Gravy.

Pour off practically all the fat from the roasting-pan into a cup or bowl. (This, when cold, makes dripping. Clarify it by pouring a little boiling water into it.) Now put the roasting-pan on top of the oven over a moderate flame and pour into it about half a pint of warm water or stock – in this case you should use the water in which the turnips have been boiled. Take a spoon and scrape every particle from the sides, bottom and corners of the pan. As you continue to do this the gravy will grow darker. Go on stirring. Taste and see if pepper and salt is needed. Bring the gravy to the boil and let it boil gently for a few minutes. Then pour it through a strainer into a really hot gravy dish.

If, on a false alarm, you make the gravy too early you should boil about half an inch of water in a frying-pan and stand the gravy dish in this, covered with a cloth, until it is wanted. Gravy must always be very hot.

RECIPE 2.

Creamed Turnips. (Cost: about 4½d.)

1 lb. turnips	Pepper, salt
1 oz. butter	Paprika
2d. worth cream	Teaspoonful vinegar

Quarter a pound of turnips (they are very tough to peel whole), peel them and then, if they are very large, cut them into eighths. Cook them for an hour in boiling, salted water with a teaspoonful of vinegar. Test them to see if they are cooked – they should be soft all through. If they are cooked, drain them thoroughly (keeping back some of the water in which they were cooked to make gravy) and chop them in the colander and mash them with a fork.

Melt an ounce of butter in a frying-pan. When it is melted and very hot add the mashed turnips and fry them for a few minutes. Add plenty of pepper and salt and stir in twopennyworth of cream. Serve the *purée* of turnips in a very hot vegetable dish and, at the last moment, sprinkle it with a little paprika.

RECIPE 3.

Cranberry and Apple Snow. (Cost: about 1/7.)

1 lb. apples (cooking)	2 ozs. castor sugar
¼ lb. cranberries	6 ozs. loaf sugar
2 eggs (whites only used)	Slices of dried lemon peel
6d. worth cream	

Buy a pound of cooking apples and a quarter of a pound of cranberries. Wash the cranberries.

Put half a teacupful of water with six ounces of loaf sugar in a saucepan and bring to the boil, stirring with a wooden spoon. When the syrup boils, add the cranberries and simmer them until they are thoroughly soft. (This will take about twenty-five minutes.) Stir with the spoon and mash against the side of the saucepan for a minute. Now put a colander in a large bowl and pour the contents of the saucepan into the colander. Mash with the spoon until all the cranberry *purée* passes through into the bowl. Set aside for a few minutes. The *purée* should amount to about a gill in quantity and be as thick as a jelly.

Peel, core, and cut up your apples into slices. Just cover the bottom of a saucepan with water and add two tablespoonfuls of castor sugar, a few pieces of dried lemon peel (which, let us hope, you have been providently storing in a tin) and the apples. Cook very gently until the apples are soft – about ten minutes – turning occasionally with the wooden spoon, so that all may be equally cooked. When the apples are soft, add the cranberry *purée*, stir all well together and continue to simmer for a few minutes longer. The mixture should be stiff rather than watery, and in fact the stiffer it is (without burning) the better for this dish. Set it aside to get cool.

Whip up sixpennyworth of cream with a whisk or fork until it is stiff. Crack two eggs against the edge of a bowl and let the whites drip down into the bowl while you turn the yolks from one half of the shell to the other until they are thoroughly free of white. Set the yolks aside to use on some other occasion.

Whip up the whites with a fork or whisk until they are very stiff and will not drop from the end of the fork.

Stir the whipped cream into the cooled apples and cranberry *purée*, not beating it, but blending it gently and thoroughly. Then add the whipped whites in the same way. The snow should be a rosy pink and exquisitely light.

Serve very cold in separate glasses for each guest.

SHOPPING LIST

					s.	d.
Butcher.						
2½ lbs. New Zealand loin of mutton, boned ready for rolling	...	...	...	...	2	6
1 oz. chopped suet	...	...	...	...	0	1
Dairy.						
3 eggs (two yolks left over)		...	...	...	0	6
Cream (one 2d. and one 6d. carton)		...	...	0	8
Greengrocer.						
1 lb. potatoes	...	...	...	...	0	1½
1 lb. turnips	...	...	...	...	0	1½
1 lb. cooking apples	...	...	...	...	0	4
¼ lb. cranberries	...	...	...	...	0	3
From Stock.						
Breadcrumbs for stuffing	...	...	...	...	0	0½
1 onion	...	...	...	...	...	0	0½
Parsley	...	...	...	...	...	0	0½
1 oz. butter for turnip	...	...	...	...	0	1
Dripping for roast	...	...	...	...	0	1
½ lb. sugar for sweet	...	...	...	...	0	1½

	5	0

Herbs, vinegar, paprika, lemon peel, negligible

DINNERS FOR BEGINNERS

TIME-TABLE

Dinner at Eight O'Clock

N.B. – If you are dining at a different hour, calculate from the time-table the hour at which you will have to start your preparations and then alter the hands of the kitchen clock to conform with the time-table. You will find this easier than making individual calculations over every item.

You had better start making the sweet early, as, unless you have some experience, your undivided attention should be given to the meat and vegetable in this menu. Begin to make the sweet at 5 o'clock. This allows an hour and a half for the sweet alone – ample time for cooling and washing up.

5 0   Make sweet. Wash up.
6 30   *Start boiling salted water for turnips.*
       Peel and cut up turnips and potatoes.
6 40   *Start boiling turnips.*
       Light oven.
       Prepare stuffing.
6 55   *Stuff mutton, roll up and tie or skewer.*
       Start cooking mutton – heat very high.
       Baste and turn occasionally.
7 10   *Lower oven heat slightly.*
       Dry potatoes and add them to meat in oven.
       Baste from time to time.

Put Plates and Dishes to warm between Oven and Hot Plate

Lay the Table

You have now nothing to do but baste occasionally until 7 40.

7 40 *Drain turnips.* (KEEP WATER.) *Chop and mash turnips in colander. Heat butter in saucepan.*

7 43 *Fry turnips in butter, add seasoning and cream.*

7 50 *Put turnips in hot dish in plate rack* above flame.

7 55 Turn oven heat very low. *Take out mutton and potatoes* put on hot dish and return to oven.

Drain off fat and make gravy in roasting-pan.

8 0 Strain gravy into hot dish.

Dust turnips with paprika.

If people are likely to be late, you had better not take out the mutton at 7. 55. Instead, you should turn the oven heat to low, take out the potatoes and put them in a hot, covered dish on the plate rack with the flame turned on below, and put on the lid of the roasting-pan. In this way you will keep the mutton really hot without overcooking it. Do not start making the gravy until your guests arrive.

Leave the turnips where they are, but do not dust with paprika until just before serving.

FILLETS OF STEAK MAITRE D'HOTEL

BAKED TOMATOES

BRUSSELS SPROUTS

BOILED POTATOES

AMY'S CRUMB PIE

The whole success of this dinner depends on your beguiling the butcher into giving you some really tender, well-hung steak. Your butcher SHOULD be one of your greatest friends, and if he is, he may do this for you. If he does not, you may as well wash the idea of this dinner from your mind, as it will only weary your guests' jaws, and drive you into the anxious apologies which, though we know them to be unsophisticated and ill-bred, will spring to our lips in moments of bitter disappointment.

Crumb pie is a recipe brought back from Canada, apparently quite unknown here, easy to make and very good.

RECIPE I.

Grilled Fillets of Steak and Watercress. (Cost: about 3/1.)

1½ lbs. English rump steak	1 bundle watercress
A very little olive oil	Pepper, salt

Buy one and a half pounds of rump steak, asking

the butcher to beat it well and to cut it not more than an inch thick.

Wipe the meat. Mix a teaspoonful of salt and a quarter of a teaspoonful of pepper together and rub the meat on both sides with the mixture. Pour a dessertspoonful of olive oil into an egg-cup and paint the seasoned meat with the oil on both sides, using a pastry brush.

Now light the grill and make it very hot. When the frets are red-hot and the grid itself very hot, place the prepared steak on the grid. Brown the steak well on one side for a minute, keeping the heat very high, then turn and brown on the other side. Now lower the heat of the grill just a little and cook the steak for about ten minutes, turning it several times so that each side is equally cooked. (Eight minutes is enough if you are sure that everyone likes their steak underdone – fifteen if they prefer it *very* well done.) When you turn the steak, use the flat sides of two knives; if you use a fork you may prick the steak and the juice will escape.

To serve, put on a VERY HOT dish, dispose small bunches of well-washed and drained watercress around, put the tomatoes at either end of the dish, and as each piece of steak is served put a piece of *maître d'hôtel* butter on top of it.

This is a dish for punctual people. If guests are late your steak will get less and less nice, though it can be kept from complete disaster by putting it in the bottom of the oven in a warm fireproof dish with the lid on, and leaving it there at the lowest possible heat.

Let the watercress and tomatoes be plentiful. Otherwise, after one helping of steak has been given, the remaining fillets will present such a meagre appearance that no one will care to take a second helping. If the dish is still well garnished, guests are apt to be less bashful; some people, too, have a strange partiality for watercress and if given half a chance will meditatively gnaw it up to the very last leaf on the dish.

RECIPE 2.
Maître d'Hôtel Butter. (Cost: about 4d.)

  1 tablespoonful chopped parsley
  2 ozs. butter
  2 tablespoonfuls lemon juice

Wash, dry and chop some parsley finely. Put two ounces of butter into a basin and work the chopped parsley and two tablespoonfuls of lemon juice into the butter with a wooden spoon. Form into pats. Keep in a very cool place till wanted.

N.B. – This should give you a line on *maître d'hôtel* sauce when you meet it in a recipe. It is made out of the same ingredients, but the butter is first melted in a saucepan and the lemon juice and parsley together with salt and pepper then added to the butter, and stirred by the edge of the stove.

RECIPE 3.
Baked Tomatoes. (Cost: about 6d.)

1 lb. small tomatoes   A little chopped parsley
A slice of onion   1 oz. butter
Salt, pepper

Buy a pound of tomatoes and wipe, but do not skin them. Cut them in halves and place them in a flat fireproof dish which you have thoroughly greased with butter.

Wash and dry some parsley and chop it finely together with a slice of onion. Sprinkle the halved tomatoes with this mixture, also with plenty of salt and pepper. Put a small piece of butter on top of each half. Bake in the oven very slowly for forty-five minutes.

You can either lift out these tomatoes from the dish and serve them at either end of the large dish on which you place the steak, or you can leave them as they are.

RECIPE 4.
Brussels Sprouts. (Cost: about 4½d.)

1½ lbs. Brussels sprouts   Salt, pepper
A very little butter

Buy a pound and a half of Brussels sprouts which should have firm, close heads and the outer leaves as little discoloured as possible. Cut off all discoloured leaves and wash the sprouts in plenty of cold, salted water.

Cook the sprouts fast in boiling salted water, with the lid of the saucepan off, for about twenty minutes. DON'T add soda, and don't cook the sprouts until they begin to fall to pieces. Lift one or two out with a knitting-needle, test and see when they are sufficiently cooked. When cooked, drain them well by shaking them vigorously in the colander and then place them in a hot vegetable dish with a sprinkling of pepper and salt, a thin slice of butter and just a dash of lemon juice scattered over the top of them.

N.B. – You must steal butter, parsley and lemon juice for this from the *maître d'hôtel* butter. It is not allowed for separately in the shopping list.

RECIPE 5.

Plain Boiled Potatoes. (Cost: about 1½d.)

    1 lb. floury potatoes   Salt

There are many delightful ways of cooking potatoes that would be appropriate here, but steak costs a lot and needs all the cook's attention, so that we must substitute 'plain boiled'. It is worth buying a packet of potato crisps and heating them in their bag in the oven, if you much prefer fried to boiled potatoes with steak. There is no reason, however, why boiled potatoes should not be extremely good, particularly if you buy the right 'floury' kind.

Peel and where possible make all the potatoes the same size, cutting large ones in halves. Put in plenty of cold, well-salted water, and bring to the boil with the lid of the saucepan off. Boil for about twenty minutes, then test with a knitting-needle or skewer. If the potatoes are done, turn them out into the colander and meantime put the saucepan back by the fire so that the moisture may evaporate from it – this will only take a few seconds. Replace the potatoes in the dry saucepan, put the saucepan by the edge of the stove and cover with a clean, dry cloth. Leave them for a minute or two and they should then be perfectly dry. Turn them out into a hot vegetable dish, and cover.

RECIPE 6.
Amy's Crumb Pie. (Cost: about 8½d.)

1½ lbs. apples	6 ozs. brown sugar
2 ozs. butter	6 ozs. flour

Buy a pound and a half of cooking apples. Peel and cut them into quarters, removing the core. Place the apples in the bottom of a fireproof dish which must be DEEP rather than flat and not too wide at the top, so that the apples may be well covered by the mixture which you now spread over them. Add no sugar to the apples and no water, but if you can spare it you may either sprinkle over a little lemon juice or mix in a good spoonful of lemon cheese.

Now blend two ounces of butter with six ounces of brown sugar in a bowl, using a fork. Work the sugar well into the butter. Next, add six ounces of sieved flour to the butter and sugar; just mix it in, you need not blend it with great care. The mixture

257

should now resemble fine breadcrumbs and be perfectly dry, leaving the sides of the bowl quite clean. Pile it on top of the apples, pressing it well down. It should be *at least an inch thick.*

Cook for about forty minutes in a slow oven, uncovered, and serve in the dish it was cooked in. The top should be a pale golden brown and rather rough, and your guests will all be sure that they know what it is and will make incorrect guesses about it.

SHOPPING LIST

					s.	d.
Butcher.						
1½ lbs. English rump steak	...	...		...	3	0
Greengrocer.						
1 lb. tomatoes	...	...	...	...	0	5
1½ lbs. Brussels sprouts	...	...	...	...	0	4½
1 lb. potatoes	...	...	...	...	0	1
1 bunch watercress	...	...	...	...	0	1
1 bunch parsley	...	...	...	...	0	1
1 lemon	...	...	...	...	0	1
1½ lbs. cooking apples	...	...	...	...	0	4½
From Stock.						
5 ozs. butter	...	...	...	...	0	4
6 ozs. flour	...	...	...	...	0	1
6 ozs. brown sugar	...	...	...	...	0	1
Olive oil, onion, salt, pepper	...	...		negligible		
					5	0

SEVEN DINNERS FOR WINTER

TIME-TABLE

DINNER AT EIGHT O'CLOCK

N.B. – If you are dining at a different hour, calculate from the time-table the hour at which you will have to start your operations and then alter the hands of the kitchen clock to conform with the time-table. You will find this easier than making individual calculations over every item.

This is emphatically not the sort of dinner which can be left to its own devices. Don't attempt it if you are very inexperienced, not because it is difficult, but because the final stages involve cooking several things at once.

6 30   LAY THE TABLE
6 50   Wash, dry and chop parsley.
        Wash and prepare Brussels sprouts. Prepare potatoes and tomatoes.
7 0   *Light the oven.*
        Start preparing crumb pie.
7 10   *Start cooking tomatoes in oven on second shelf.*
        Continue preparing crumb pie.
7 20   *Start cooking crumb pie in oven on top shelf.*
        Start boiling salted water for Brussels sprouts.

PUT PLATES AND DISHES TO WARM ON RACK. COVER WITH CLOTH

        Make *maître d'hôtel* butter. Put in a very cool place.
7 30   *Start boiling Brussels sprouts.*
        Start boiling potatoes.
        Wash and drain watercress.
7 40   *Light grill.*
        Prepare steak for grilling.

7 45   *Start grilling steak.*

7 46   *Turn steak.*

7 47   *Turn down grill heat very slightly. Continue grilling steak and turn occasionally.*

7 50   *Test sprouts. Drain and dry.* Put in hot dish with butter, pepper, salt. Cover.

7 55   *Test potatoes. Drain. Dry saucepan, return potatoes to saucepan.* Set near flame.

7 57   *Turn oven to lowest heat.*

       Turn out grill. Put steak on hot dish in bottom of oven and cover.

8 0   Put potatoes in hot dish. Cover.

       Arrange tomatoes and watercress on dish with steak. Add a piece of *maître d'hôtel* butter to each piece of steak. Turn out oven, and take out crumb pie. It is so very hot that, unless it is removed to a rather cooler place while the first course is being eaten, it will burn everyone's mouth. Do not, of course, let it get really cold.

If people are late, the potatoes and sprouts can remain where they are – leave flames burning below the rack where they are standing.

Leave the tomatoes in their dish, do not add them to the steak until the last minute.

Do not turn out the oven heat, but keep it very low indeed and have the steak well covered. Whatever you do, don't add the watercress and *maître d'hôtel* butter until the very last moment.

The crumb pie can remain where it is.

This is not a good meal to keep waiting.

ROAST RIBS OF BEEF
ROAST POTATOES
BRAISED ENDIVE

CARAMEL CUSTARD

This is a good, safe, conventional meal – easy to cook, serve and carve. Nothing but the gravy has to be done at the last moment.

Recipe 1.
Roast Ribs of Beef and Roast Potatoes. (Cost: about 3/6.)

> 3 lbs. rolled ribs of beef   1½ lbs. potatoes
> A little lard, if necessary (See recipe)

The butcher will bone and roll the beef for you and send you the bones, from which you can make an excellent stock to use for vegetable soup and as a basis for the gravy.

Peel the potatoes and cut large ones in two. Wipe them perfectly dry.

Put the beef in a roasting-pan and surround it with the peeled potatoes. If there is very little fat on the beef, put a little lard on each potato.

Make your oven really hot and put the beef and potatoes in. After five minutes, open the oven, tilt the roaster a little so that the fat runs down into one corner, scoop it up in a capacious spoon and pour it over the meat *and the potatoes*. Then lower the heat a little, keeping the oven hot, but not fierce, and continue to cook for another fifty minutes, or one hour in all (for a joint three pounds in weight. If it weighs more, allow another fifteen minutes for every pound). Repeat the basting process three more times, about every fifteen minutes, and see that the potatoes get their good share of fat. Turn them from time to time so that they are browned all over. If they are allowed to get dry they will have skins like brick, through which knife and fork can scarcely crash. (If they appear to be getting very hard, and you feel helpless about preventing it, take them out as soon as they are brown and put them in a steamer over a saucepan of boiling water to finish them. But this is not likely to happen in this particular case.)

When the meat and potatoes are done, put them on a hot dish, together, and keep them warm in the oven, with the heat turned off, while you make the gravy.

Gravy.

When you put the meat in the oven, or before, if you can find time, put the bones in a saucepan with plenty of water, to which a little pepper and salt has been added. Simmer very gently on a low flame all the time the meat is cooking.

If you have not received the bones from the butcher, you can perfectly well use hot water instead, but tell him to give you the bones next time.

To make the gravy, pour nearly all the fat from

the roasting-pan in which the meat was cooked into an enamel vessel (you might crack a china one with the boiling fat) and put the roasting-pan, with the remains of the fat (about a tablespoonful) on a low flame. With a wooden spoon, stir and scrape the bits of meat from the side and bottom of the pan. Then add to the sizzling fat, hot stock from the bones (or, if you have none, hot water) until you have sufficient gravy. Stir and scrape all the time until the pan is quite clean at sides and bottom – the little bits of meat and juice clinging to the sides are invaluable both for colour and taste. There is never any need to add browning matter for colouring beef gravy, if you do this thoroughly.

When the pan is clean and the gravy boiling, pour it into a *hot* gravy boat or jug. Gravy cools very quickly, and when cool is horrid, so that if your gravy boat is very open and gets quickly chilled, throw convention to the winds and serve the gravy in a narrow-necked jug.

Do not make the gravy until just before you are ready to eat, if possible. But if you have to keep it waiting, put it in its container over a bowl of gently-boiling water, or stand it in a pan of water over a low flame.

RECIPE 2.
Braised Endive. (Cost: about 8½d.)
        1 lb. endive

It is the white endive which is sometimes called chicory which you need for this dish – not the curly salad variety. It is usually sold by the pound, but sometimes by the bundle – in which case a bundle is about the quantity you require.

Wash it well, removing any outer leaves which may be dirty or blemished. Trim the root a little, and put the endive very carefully into boiling salted water in a saucepan large enough to take it lying down. Add a squeeze of lemon juice, and boil gently for five minutes.

Now take the endive out and drain it carefully in a colander. It is a very tender vegetable and easily bruised, so be circumspect in the way you handle it. Put it in a fireproof dish with some butter (about an ounce), pepper and salt. Close the lid and, holding it firmly in position, shake the dish well to distribute the butter – which will melt slightly almost at once on the hot endive.

Cook in the oven for about half an hour. Serve the endive in the casserole. It will look semi-transparent when done, and a greenish-white.

You are cooking this with the meat in a rather hot oven, but if you should cook it in a cooler oven, allow it another quarter of an hour. Slow braising is always best, if you can arrange it.

RECIPE 3.
Caramel Custard. (Cost: about 1/–.)

2 ozs. loaf sugar	4 eggs Pinch of salt
2 tablespoonfuls water	A little vanilla essence
½ pint milk	½ oz. castor sugar

Make a caramel by putting two ounces of loaf

sugar with two tablespoonfuls of water in a saucepan, and bringing it slowly to the boil. Stir or shake
all the time, and continue to boil fairly rapidly until
it becomes coffee-coloured.

Coat a dry tin charlotte mould with the caramel
by pouring in the mixture and turning the mould
about so that it runs into every part. Leave it to set
while you make the custard.

Heat half a pint of milk with a few drops of vanilla
and a pinch of salt until it is nearly boiling, in a
double-lipped saucepan, if you have one. As soon as
a sort of skin forms on the top and the surface of the
milk seems to rise a little, take it off the fire.

Separate the yolks from the whites of two eggs by
cracking the eggs against the side of a basin and
letting the whites drip down while you turn the
yolks from one half of the egg to the other. Take the
two yolks and two whole eggs and slightly beat them
with a dessertspoonful of sugar. Put them in the top
of a double boiler over boiling water.

Pour the hot, but not boiling, milk on to the eggs,
stirring, as you pour, with a wooden spoon. Go on
stirring over gentle heat until the custard thickens
and seems heavy on the spoon. Take it off the fire
and go on stirring over the steaming water in the
lower part of the boiler until it has the consistency of
thick cream. You must be careful to take it off the
flame the moment it thickens, or you will overshoot
the mark.

Feel your caramel lightly with the tip of your

finger to make quite sure that it is set firmly. Pour in the custard and tie a piece of greaseproof paper over the top of the mould.

Cook *au bain marie* – that is, stand your mould in a pan of boiling water in a fairly slow oven – for about an hour, or until the custard is firm in the centre.

When it is done, let it cool for a few moments before turning it out.

If you want the caramel to remain hard, keep it in a cool place until you are ready to serve it. Otherwise it will become soft and run down the sides. But this is merely a matter of taste.

SHOPPING LIST

	s.	d.
Butcher.		
3 lbs ribs of beef (chilled)	3	0
Dairy.		
½ pint milk	0	1¾
4 eggs	0	8
Greengrocer.		
1½ lbs. potatoes	0	2
1 lb. endive	0	8
1 lemon	0	1½
From Stock.		
3 ozs. loaf sugar	0	0½
1 oz. butter for endive	0	1
1 oz. lard for potatoes	0	0½
Vanilla essence	negligible	
	4	11¼

SEVEN DINNERS FOR WINTER

TIME-TABLE

Dinner at Eight O'Clock

N.B. – If you are dining at a different hour, calculate from the time-table the hour at which you will have to start your preparations and then alter the hands of the kitchen clock to conform with the time-table. You will find this easier than making individual calculations over every item.

———————

This is a meal devoid of rush in preparation. You must make the pudding first and cook it before starting the rest of the meal, as the oven in which you will cook the meat will be much too hot for the caramel. You should allow yourself about 30 minutes for making the sweet, and 60 to cook it. This will leave the sweet an hour and twenty minutes to cool.

5 10   *Make caramel custard.*
        (Do not forget to light the oven at 5. 25.)
5 40   *Put caramel custard in oven.*
             Wash up
         Lay the Table
6 15   Peel potatoes, wash and dry them.
        Wash endive.
6 35   Put meat and potatoes in pan ready to put in oven.
6 40   *Take out sweet and put in cool place.*
        Turn up heat ready for meat.
6 55   *Put meat in oven.*
7 0   Baste meat and lower oven heat.
7 15   Baste meat.
7 20   *Put on salted water to boil for endive.*
7 25   *Put endive in boiling water.*

267

7 30   *Put endive, drained, in fireproof dish with butter in oven.*
      Baste meat.

   PUT PLATES AND DISHES ON TOP OF OVEN TO HEAT
      (Change the plates round occasionally, as other-
      wise only the lower ones will get really hot.)

7 55   *Take meat out of oven and dish up with potatoes.*
      Put back in oven, with heat turned low, to keep hot.
      Put any plates or dishes which are not really hot in
        oven.
      Make gravy.
      Serve endive in dish in which it was cooked.

If people are late, put the lid of the roasting-pan on, turn down the heat and leave it. Leave the endive where it is. The sweet is cold in any case. Delay making the gravy until you can serve the meal.

BOEUF A LA BOURGEOISE
(Beef Stewed with Olives)

BAKED TOMATOES
POTATOES BAKED IN THEIR JACKETS

TREACLE TART

Hot sweets have been deliberately excluded from many of the menus in this book. A majority of people to-day prefer light, cold sweets, generally made from some kind of fruit, and these, incidentally, are the easiest for a single-handed hostess to serve. Sometimes, however, on a cold winter's day, appetite rebels and clamours for a hot, sustaining pudding. Treacle tart is an old favourite, easy to make and easy to keep waiting when people are late.

Why should potatoes baked in their jackets be almost invariably forced into company with cold meat? Serve them in this menu with the hot meat, but give each of your guests a hot side plate and let him deal with the potatoes on this as he may. See that there is PLENTY OF BUTTER ON THE TABLE.

RECIPE 1.

Bœuf à la Bourgeoise. (Cost: about 3/4½.)

    2 lbs. beef without bone (English topside or stewing
      steak)
    ¼ lb. butter
    1 small tin of olives
    Pepper, salt

Consult your butcher, telling him that you want
two pounds of beef without bone and with as little
fat as possible. A very small joint of topside would do,
or a piece of stewing steak cut thickly. Do not buy ribs
or sirloin. Beat the meat on both sides with a rolling
pin in order to make it as tender as possible.

Put a quarter of a pound of butter to heat in a
saucepan. When it is hissing hot, put in the meat and
fry it for a few minutes on either side, until it is well
browned. Then add pepper and salt and close down
the lid of the saucepan tightly over a piece of greaseproof paper. Leave to simmer over a very low heat
for two hours.

While the meat is cooking, turn out the contents of
a tin of olives (you can buy these cheaply from certain
fishmongers) and throw away the liquid. Stone
the olives by peeling the flesh away from the stone –
go round and round the olive with a small, sharp
knife as though you were peeling an orange. Throw
away the stones and, twenty minutes before the
meat is due to be ready for the table, add the flesh
of the olives. Close the lid down firmly again and
continue cooking at the same heat.

To serve, lift out the meat and carve it into slices. Lay these slices overlapping one another in a hot dish. Place the olives on top and pour over the gravy from the bottom of the saucepan.

RECIPE 2.
Baked Tomatoes. (Cost: about 7½d.)

> 1 lb. (or just over) tomatoes   A little parsley
> 1 oz. butter   A slice of onion
> Salt, pepper

Buy at least four large tomatoes – they will probably weigh a bit more than a pound. Wipe them but do not skin them. Cut them in halves and place them in a flat fireproof dish well greased with butter.

Wash and dry some parsley and pick it from the stalks. Cut a slice from an onion and chop it finely, together with the parsley. Sprinkle the halved tomatoes with the mixed onion and parsley, and add a very little salt and pepper. Put a little piece of butter on the top of each half. Bake in the oven, uncovered, at low heat for from forty to forty-five minutes.

RECIPE 3.
Potatoes Baked in their Jackets. (Cost: about 3d.)

> 4 large potatoes

Tell the greengrocer that you want four large potatoes of equal size for baking in their jackets. They will probably cost about threepence. Wash them well, scrubbing off every bit of dirt, if necessary, with a nail brush. Dry them. Make a slit with a knife in each – this will prevent them bursting as they cook. If any are decidedly larger than the others, grease them all over and they will cook more quickly than they would otherwise do. Place them in the oven – you need not put them on a plate or dish, just rest them on the bars of a shelf – and cook at very low heat for about two hours. Turn them from time to time. When they are cooked, they should feel soft and yielding when you press them with your hand. They should not be burnt black. If they are cooked too soon, take them out and keep them in a warm place or put them at the extreme bottom of the oven.

Serve, if possible, in a wooden bowl.

RECIPE 4.
Treacle Tart. (Cost: about 5½d.)

    Half a 1 lb. tin of golden syrup
    1 lemon
    2 or 3 tablespoonfuls of breadcrumbs
    6 ozs. flour
    3 ozs. lard
    ¼ teaspoonful baking powder
    1 tablespoonful water
    Pinch of salt

Crumble some slices of white bread without crust in a basin until you have from two to three tablespoonfuls of crumbs. Grate the outer skin of a lemon into the crumbs, and add the juice of half a lemon, strained. Now add half the contents of a pound tin of golden syrup and stir all together. If possible, leave standing all night.

Lightly flour the inside of a round flat tin. Now make some *short pastry*.

Sieve six ounces of flour with a pinch of salt through a sieve or strainer into a big bowl. Break up three ounces of lard into small bits, put these into the flour and rub them into it lightly and quickly with the tips of your fingers. When all the shortening is rubbed into the flour, it should look like breadcrumbs. Make a little hole in the middle of this and add about a dessertspoonful of water. Mix it in quickly with a pastry-knife. Add another dessertspoonful of water and mix in again. You should now have a stiff paste. Knead this with the knuckles of your hand until it forms a firm ball of dough that leaves the side of the basin quite clean. Turn out on to a well-floured board and knead again for a minute – this second kneading should make the dough absolutely firm and cohesive so that it does not split when rolled.

Flour your rolling-pin well and roll out the pastry. Roll it lightly and quickly in one direction and, in order to get it a round shape, keep turning it to your left on the board and rolling away from you that portion that is directly in front of you. If it starts splitting you must gather it all up into a ball, give it a little more kneading – which is what it needs –

273

and roll it out again. When it is about the size you want, lay the floured tin, face downwards on the pastry, and cut all round about half an inch beyond its edge with the knife. Take away the tin, lift the pastry with the help of the pastry-knife and ease it into the tin. Cut the edges at regular intervals with the knife and bend one section forward, the next back – or turn in the edge in a roll and mark it in a pattern with the knife. Prick the bottom in several places with a fork and pour in the prepared treacle. Some people now roll out the trimmings of pastry left on the board, cut them into strips, roll these by hand into cords and fix them across the tart. Do this, if you like, but remember that guests may be depressed to get a helping of tart that is all strips of decorative pastry with treacle in a sad minority.

Cook in a quick oven for twenty-five minutes or until the pastry is golden colour. When cooked, take the tart out of the oven and, if you can manage this without breaking it, slip it off the tin on to a clean, hot plate. The tart will remain extremely hot for some time if kept in a warm part of the kitchen.

SEVEN DINNERS FOR WINTER

SHOPPING LIST

		s.	d.
Butcher.			
2 lbs English beef without bone		2	6
Fishmonger or Delicatessen.			
1 small tin of olives		0	7½
Greengrocer.			
4 large tomatoes – probably just over 1 lb. ...		0	6
4 large potatoes – between 2 and 3 lbs... ...		0	3
1 lemon		0	1
From Stock.			
5 ozs. butter – for beef and tomatoes		0	5
6 ozs. flour		0	0½
3 ozs. lard		0	1½
Half a 1 lb. tin of golden syrup		0	3
Breadcrumbs, parsley		0	0½
		4	10

TIME-TABLE

DINNER AT EIGHT O'CLOCK

N.B. – If you are dining at a different time, calculate from the time-table at what hour you will have to start your preparations and then alter the hands of the kitchen clock to conform with the time-table. You will find it easier than making individual calculations over every item.

———

5 40   Scrub, dry and prick potatoes.
5 50   *Light oven.*
5 54   *Heat butter for beef in saucepan.*

5 55   *Start frying beef,* turn once.

6 0   *Close down lid of saucepan and start cooking beef at very low heat. Start baking potatoes in top of oven at very low heat.*

LAY THE TABLE

BEYOND THE FACT THAT YOU MUST OCCASIONALLY TURN THE POTATOES, YOU ARE NOW FREE FOR AN HOUR

7 0   Grease a flat fireproof dish and flour a flat round tin.

Wipe tomatoes, cut in halves, put on dish.

Wash and dry parsley, chop with onion, add to tomatoes.

Season tomatoes, dot with butter.

7 15   *Start cooking tomatoes in oven,* just below potatoes.

Start making pastry for treacle tart.

7 30   *Turn up oven to quick heat.* Move potatoes and tomatoes to bottom of oven.

Line floured tin with pastry, prick, pour in treacle mixture and decorate.

7 35   *Start cooking treacle tart in quick oven* (top).

PUT PLATES AND DISHES TO WARM

Stone olives.

7 40   *Add olives to beef.*

7 59   *Take out treacle tart,* put on plate-rack, turn oven down as low as possible.

8 0   *Take out beef from saucepan, carve and arrange on hot dish.* Pour gravy over.

Take out potatoes and tomatoes, turn out oven.

Leave the treacle tart where it is and slip it off on to a warm plate (with the help of a pastry-knife) just before serving.

If guests are late, leave everything as it is, treacle tart on plate-rack, beef in saucepan, potatoes and tomatoes in the oven.

Cover the tomatoes.

ONION SOUP

COQUILLES ST. JACQUES
(Scallops)

BAKED LEMON APPLES

Here is a fish dinner for a cold night. The soup is
very nourishing and easy to prepare. Coquilles St.
Jacques is a French way of cooking scallops and so
excellent that once you have tried your hand at it
you will want to cook it again and again. The
simple sweet is very familiar, but has a variation
in flavouring.

RECIPE 1.
Onion Soup. (Cost: about 4d.)

2 medium onions	1½ pints water
2 ozs. butter	Pepper, salt
2 ozs. grated cheese	

Peel and chop two medium-sized onions. Melt
an ounce of butter in a saucepan and when it is very
hot add the onions. Fry the onions, stirring them
with a wooden spoon so that they do not burn, for
about ten minutes – they should be a golden-brown.
Add a pint and a half of hot water and a dessertspoonful of salt to the onions and bring very gradually to the boil. This will take from fifteen to twenty

minutes, perhaps less. When the liquid boils, pour it through a colander into a large bowl, passing as much of the onion as possible through the colander with the back of the spoon. Now pour back the liquid into the saucepan and bring it gently to the boil again. Add about two ounces of grated cheese (any common kind that you can keep dry in your store-cupboard will do). Taste and add pepper and more salt if necessary.

Simmer the soup for ten minutes or so. Then put a small piece of butter in a warm bowl and pour the boiling soup over it. Stir well and serve very hot in little marmite pots or small soup bowls. In Paris, where this soup is very popular, it is thickened with pieces of bread or toast, and very good it is. But this would be almost too filling a way of beginning a meal unless one were exceedingly hungry.

RECIPE 2.

Coquilles St. Jacques. (Cost: about 3/7.)

4 large scallops	2 ozs. butter
¼ lb. mushrooms	1 oz. flour
1 onion	1 tablespoonful stale crumbs
1 tomato	Pepper, salt
	A little parsley

Buy four scallops and try to persuade the fish-monger to give you four of his most curved scallop shells to serve them in. The scallops should have bright orange-coloured centres and clean outer whites, and should look like large, clean and freshly-poached eggs. They will vary from about fourpence to eightpence each, according to size. Allow one large scallop for each person, or, if the shell-fish are very small, two for each person.

Wash them well and put them into plenty of boiling salted water. Boil, not too fast, for about ten minutes. Meanwhile, chop an onion, some washed, dried parsley and a quarter of a pound of peeled mushrooms (including the stalks, if these are good). Pour a little boiling water over a tomato so that the skin comes away easily; peel the tomato and chop it coarsely.

Drain the scallops, but do not throw away the water in which they were cooked. Chop them thoroughly, red and white parts together, and mix them with the chopped mushrooms, onion, tomato and parsley in a bowl. Add a dessertspoonful of salt and a good sprinkling of pepper.

Melt an ounce of butter in a saucepan and when it is very hot add everything from the bowl and cook all together in the butter for a few minutes, stirring with a wooden spoon so that nothing may burn. Then cover the saucepan and set it at the edge of the stove to keep warm while you make the sauce that is to bind it.

Melt another ounce of butter in a saucepan. When it is melted and very hot stir into it a tablespoonful of flour. The mixture will be very thick. Take the saucepan to the edge of the stove and add gradually, stirring all the time, about a teacup and a half of the water in which you boiled the scallops. Keep on stirring steadily until the sauce is smooth, then return the saucepan to the flame and bring the sauce to the boil, still stirring; if it is almost solid, add a little more of the scallop water. Let the sauce boil gently all over for about five minutes. Taste and see if it needs any more seasoning and add some if it does.

It will take you about fifteen minutes to make this sauce. When it is made, pour it over the scallops, etc., in the other saucepan and stir them all thoroughly together. The result should be a rich, dark – almost black – substance; grease the scallop shells and fill them with the mixture. Scatter over the top of each a sprinkling of fine stale crumbs, made by drying odds and ends of bread in a very slow oven and then crushing them to crumbs with a rolling-pin. Put the shells, uncovered, into a moderate oven to finish cooking for fifteen minutes. (If you have no shells, put the mixture into a flattish fireproof dish.)

Slices of finely-cut brown bread and butter taste excellent with this dish.

RECIPE 3.
Baked Lemon Apples. (Cost: about 1/0½.)

4 large cooking apples	Juice of 1 lemon
or 8 small ones	A few stoned raisins
2 ozs. butter	Very small pinch of cinnamon
4 ozs. brown sugar	

Buy four large cooking apples or eight smaller

ones. They must be unblemished and of a good kind. Wipe them carefully but do not peel them.

Squeeze out the juice of a lemon and strain it into a bowl. Add two tablespoonfuls of brown sugar, two ounces of butter, and a tiny pinch of cinnamon. Work all this together with the back of a wooden spoon until it is well blended. If some of the lemon juice is still unblended, never mind.

Core your apples, taking care not to break them. If you have not got an apple corer, take a sharp knife and mark a small square round the place where the stalk grows. Now place the tip of the knife on each side of the square in turn, cutting right down until the tip of the blade appears at the other end of the apple. When you have done this, take the apple firmly in your left hand and push down where the square is marked with your right thumb. The centre of the apple will come out in a solid piece, including the core.

Stand the cored apples in a fireproof dish. Fill the hollowed-out centres nearly to the top with the prepared lemon mixture. Into the top of each hollow stuff a few cleaned, stoneless raisins from the packet which you should have in your store-cupboard. Pour about half a teacupful of warm water round the apples – there should be about a quarter of an inch of water in the dish – add two tablespoonfuls of brown sugar to the water.

Leave the apples uncovered and bake them very slowly in the oven for an hour. Baste them occasionally with the liquid in the bottom of the dish (i.e., lift the liquid in a spoon and pour it over the apples). They should be soft all through when finished, but not split and collapsing in squashy heaps. Look at them from time to time, and if they are cooking too fast, turn down the oven heat.

Serve in the dish in which they were cooked.

SHOPPING LIST

	s.	d.
Fishmonger.		
4 large scallops (or 8 small ones), with shells ...	2	6
Dairy.		
6 ozs. butter	0	5
Greengrocer.		
1 lb. onions (for soup and scallops)	0	1½
¼ lb. mushrooms	0	7½
2 lbs. cooking apples	0	8
1 lemon	0	1
From Stock.		
2 ozs. cheese	0	1
1 tomato, a little parsley	0	1
1 tablespoonful stale crumbs	0	0½
A few raisins	0	0½
4 ozs. brown sugar	0	1
	4	**9**

Flour, cinnamon, negligible.

SEVEN DINNERS FOR WINTER

TIME-TABLE

DINNER AT EIGHT O'CLOCK

N.B. – If you are dining at a different time, calculate from the time-table the hour at which you will have to start your preparations and then alter the hands of the kitchen clock to conform with the time-table. You will find this easier than making individual calculations over every item.

Beforehand: If you have no stale crumbs stored in tins, then make some by drying scraps of bread in a very slow oven and crushing them with the rolling-pin.

5 30   LAY THE TABLE

5 40   Prepare apples for baking. Fill with mixture, arrange in dish and set aside. (Do not pour water and sugar round until just before baking.)

6 0   Grate cheese.
Wipe, peel, and chop mushrooms.
Wash, dry and chop parsley.
Peel and chop tomato.
Peel and chop onions for soup and scallops.

6 20   *Start heating water for soup.*
Start frying onions for soup.

6 30   *Add hot water to onions,* bring to the boil.

6 45   *Pass onion soup through colander,* return to saucepan and set aside.

6 50   *Light oven.*
Start boiling salted water for scallops.
Wash scallops.

7 0   *Start cooking apples in slow oven, top shelf.*
Start cooking scallops in boiling water.
Put on soup to heat through and simmer very gently.

283

DINNERS FOR BEGINNERS

Put Plates and Marmite Pots to Warm between Oven
and Grill. If there is not enough room some may go on
the Rack covered with a Cloth

7 15   *Drain scallops*, keep water.
       Chop scallops, mix with mushrooms, etc.
       Heat butter in saucepan.
       Cook scallops, etc., in butter. Season.

7 25   *Set scallops, etc., at edge of stove,* covered.
       Start making sauce.

7 42   *Bind scallops, etc., with sauce.* Put mixture in shells,
       scatter crumbs over.
       *Raise oven to moderate heat, put apples on lower shelf,
       and start cooking scallops on top shelf.*

7 45   *Add grated cheese to soup.*

8 0   *Put lump of butter in warm bowl, pour soup over, stir well*
       and pour into marmite pots.
       Turn oven down to lowest possible heat. Leave
       scallops and apples in oven, covered, and put
       plates on bottom shelf.

If people are late you can keep the soup hot indefinitely.
Do not pour it over the butter until just before you serve it.
The apples and scallops will not be hurt by a little extra
cooking; but you had better cover them.

CHAPTER VII

IMPROMPTU MEALS

THE mainstay of the impromptu meal is the tin, out of which comes the only food that can be guaranteed to meet emergencies. You cannot always have butter, eggs, flour or 'left-overs' in the house, but you can and must always have a few tins. Then, whether you are returning home from a holiday to an empty larder, or have been driven home early by pouring rain on a chilly Sunday, you can keep a smiling face towards hungry people.

Impromptu meals must be capable of easy and quick preparation while your family screams for food or your guests hollowly protest that you must not trouble. It is as well to perfect oneself in the cooking of a dish that is a general favourite and then to keep the ingredients permanently in the store-cupboard. You will not have it often enough to get tired of it, and some familiarity with the cooking involved will make for ease and speed in preparation.

Some suggestions follow for meals that come entirely out of tins. A good look at the catalogue of one of the big stores will very likely give you fresh ideas of your own. After the tinned recipes come a few which need eggs, butter, flour or milk, which may

285

possibly lurk in your larder. We will not assume that you have anything else in the house.

One word more before we come to business. Some people honestly like such things as salmon and sardines straight out of the tin. Do not deny them this simple pleasure and insist on sacrificing them to your ingenuity. But also pay attention to the infinite possibilities of disguise and remember that something hot will very often save the life of your party.

Soups. – Tinned soups are excellent. Always have a large tin in the house. If it is a clear or vegetable soup, it can be increased in quantity by the addition of water; if a cream soup like tomato or celery, add unsweetened tinned milk, several small tins of which should always be in the house as a precaution against a thousand emergencies.

Cream soups can be used undiluted as a sauce. Celery or asparagus soup makes an excellent white sauce to serve with fish.

A good soup can be made from a tin of tomato *purée*, which is very cheap, to which a small tin of milk and a breakfastcupful of water has been added.

When adding milk to a cream soup, open the tin and pour the contents into a saucepan. Bring slowly to the boil. Meanwhile, warm the milk, or milk and water, but do not let it boil. When the soup is thoroughly hot and bubbling gently, add the warm milk and do not let the mixture boil again.

When adding water to a tinned soup, it should be previously heated.

Fish. – Salmon, sardines, lobster, crab, prawns, herrings can all be had in tinned form, and whilst they can be eaten straight out of the tin, they can also be successfully dressed up according to the recipes which you will find on page 288 *et seq.*, or to others which your own ingenuity will devise.

Meat. – If meat is your object, tinned chicken can now be obtained quite cheaply embedded in a jelly which can be made into soup or served cold. Tongue, ham and galantines provide time-honoured stand-bys. They can be served cold with a good vegetable salad from another tin.

Vegetables. – Tinned vegetables of all kinds, including potatoes, spinach, peas, beans, mushrooms, asparagus, carrots and tomatoes are becoming better every year. Tinned English vegetables of all varieties are particularly good. They are rather expensive, but the emergency tin does not make a very frequent appearance on the bills.

Fruit. – Everyone is only too familiar with tinned fruit, but it is possible to find the less hackneyed varieties and vary their preparation. Cherries, plums and strawberries are less common than the everlasting fruit salad, pineapple and peach.

Savouries. – Spaghetti, baked beans and mushrooms are good, reviving dishes when they are served hot.

If you so desire, it is, of course, possible nowadays to have all the ingredients of a conventional meal from tins (which makes one wonder why it is that so many English country hotels are outraged by the idea of a hot meal after eight or nine o'clock at night). But, on the whole, you will probably find your emergencies better served by odd dishes, for which some recipes follow.

RECIPE 1.
Salmon with Tomatoes and Pimento.

Turn the salmon out of the tin and remove the bone. Put it into a fireproof dish and pour over it the fruit from a large tin of tomatoes together with about a third of the liquid. Add the contents of a small tin of pimento (costing about 5½d.), disposing the strips of pimento neatly about the dish. Cover and bake for about fifteen minutes in a moderate oven, until piping hot. Serve on hot plates.

RECIPE 2.
Salmon with Cream Sauce and Peas.

Turn the salmon out of the tin and remove the bone. Put it into a small saucepan and stir over a gentle heat. When it is well broken up and hot, turn it out into a hot dish and cover with the undiluted contents of a tin of celery soup which has been previously heated in a saucepan. Meanwhile, heat a tin of peas, according to the directions on the tin (some require heating in their tins, others require draining first). Surround the salmon and sauce on the dish with small piles of peas, and serve very hot.

RECIPE 3.
Ham, Tomatoes and Spinach.

Turn the contents of a tin of tomatoes into a fire-proof dish with the tinned ham. Bake uncovered in a moderate oven for about fifteen minutes. Meanwhile, heat the spinach in a saucepan (which can be obtained in leaf or *purée* form, whichever you prefer). If you have any butter in the house, put a small piece in the saucepan with the spinach. If not, never mind. The spinach can be served separately or on the same dish as the ham and tomato.

RECIPE 4.
Ham, Sweet Corn and Tomatoes.

Open a tin of ham and cut it up into small portions. Heat the contents of a tin of sweet corn in a saucepan, together with the contents of a small tin of tomatoes. Put a layer of this in a fireproof dish, cover with ham, and then with another layer of corn and tomatoes. Bake in a moderate oven for fifteen minutes.

RECIPE 5.
Prawns with Spaghetti.

Heat in a saucepan the contents of a large tin of spaghetti and tomato sauce, stirring constantly. Arrange in individual ramekin dishes, one for each person, and border each with a ring of prawns. Put into the oven for a few minutes to heat through thoroughly.

RECIPE 6.
Baked Beans with Tomatoes.

Open a tin of beans and turn it into a saucepan. Open a tin of tomatoes and strain the liquid, or some of it, into the beans. Do not put so much that the beans are awash, but add sufficient to prevent them sticking to the bottom of the pan while they are cooking. Meanwhile, stand the tin of tomatoes containing the whole tomatoes in a saucepan of boiling water and leave it there for ten minutes or so over a low flame, or beside a burner, while you are heating the beans gradually. When they are all hot – you will need constantly to stir and turn the beans about or the lower ones will be hot before the top – turn the beans into a dish, cover with the tomatoes, and serve.

RECIPE 7.
Lobster with Asparagus.

Heat the asparagus in the tin by piercing the top of the tin in two places and standing it in a pan of boiling water over a low heat for ten minutes. Open the tin at the *top* – the asparagus will have been packed head downwards, so that the base of the stalks will confront you when you open the lid. Let them drop gently into a hot dish. Keep warm. Now heat some asparagus soup undiluted, stirring all the while. Open the tin of lobster and turn the contents into the soup. Stir gently, until it is heated through. Serve with the asparagus.

RECEIPT 8.
Roast Chicken, Tinned New Potatoes and Tinned Beans.

If you feel you want a real meal and do not mind the extra expense, you can achieve a first-class imitation by serving a whole roasted chicken from a tin together with tinned potatoes and peas or beans. An excellent soup can be made out of the jelly in which the chicken is packed.

The chicken is heated in the tin by piercing a hole in the top and then placing the tin in boiling water for fifteen minutes. The tin is then opened and the chicken strained into a bowl to catch the liquid for soup. As a rule it is tender to the point of falling to pieces, so that great care must be exercised in handling it. The tinned potatoes, peas and beans are cooked and need only to be heated.

The chicken can, of course, be treated in other ways, or eaten cold in its jelly.

RECIPE 9.
Fruit.

Tinned fruit can be made more interesting by heating the contents of the tin in a saucepan and serving with tinned unsweetened milk or cream.

RECIPE 10.
Fruit Fool.

When you want a change from plain fruit, drain the syrup from a tin of soft fruit and mash it up with a fork, or rub it through a sieve. Stir in the contents of a tin of condensed milk or cream and serve in custard cups. This is a particularly good way with plums – the stones must, of course, be taken away.

Here are a few dishes which require eggs, milk, flour or butter, some of which may well be found in the house.

RECIPE I.
Creamed Fish on Toast.

This involves making a good white sauce.

First open your tin of fish (any fish will do) and strain the liquor into a vessel. Then to make your *white sauce*: Take an ounce of butter and melt it in a perfectly clean saucepan over a gentle flame. When it is frothing, add an ounce of flour (a heaped tablespoonful) and blend flour and butter well together with a wooden spoon. Take your saucepan to the side of the fire and add very gradually, a little at a time, a teacupful of milk and a teacupful of fish liquor which have been previously mixed together and warmed. When all the liquid is added, return to the flame and cook for five or six minutes, *stirring constantly*. The sauce must be cooked for at least this length of time, during which it must be bubbling gently, and it must be constantly stirred. Less time in cooking will result in the flour being raw and tasting like wallpaper paste. Any cessation in stirring will mean lumps and burns. Even if you are cooking in a double boiler, you must stir to guard against lumps.

When the sauce is done, add the fish and stir all together. Keep it hot in the saucepan while you make some toast, if you have any bread. (If not, serve on very hot plates.) Butter the toast and pile the creamy mixture on it.

Other things beside fish can be creamed in this way, including mushrooms.

RECIPE 2.
Corn Beef Hash.

Melt a little butter in a frying-pan and add the contents of a tin of corn beef, cut up small, salt and pepper and two tablespoonfuls of tinned tomato *purée*, and a teaspoonful of tarragon vinegar. Add a tablespoonful of water if the mixture is too dry. Simmer on a low gas, turning with a spoon from time to time for about half an hour. Serve with tomatoes, peas, beans, or any other tinned vegetable you like.

The remainder of the tin of tomato *purée* can be made into a soup with tinned milk or water.

RECIPE 3.
Sardines on Toast.

Put a little of the oil from the tin in a frying-pan, make it really hot and then fry the sardines in it. They will only take a very few minutes. Make some toast and butter it. Pile on the sardines with plenty of pepper and salt and serve at once.

RECIPE 4.
Scrambled Eggs.

This common dish is so often badly made that a reliable recipe may not be out of place.

A double boiler is a tremendous help in turning out good scrambled eggs, but if you have not got one at hand, it is perfectly possible to do without it.

Break the eggs (two for each person) into a basin and beat them lightly with some salt and pepper. Melt a very little butter – as much as you can pick up on the end of a knife at a single cut is enough – and when it is frothing in the saucepan pour in the eggs from the basin. Do not add milk or bread-crumbs or any other substance to the eggs, but if there is much egg left on the side of the basin after pouring into the saucepan, you can wash it off with a teaspoonful of milk and add it to the rest. Now stir, stir, stir, with a wooden spoon until the egg is creamy and begins to set. See that your spoon is really touching the bottom of the saucepan with every revolution. As soon as the egg is of the right consistency, whip it out on to hot buttered toast or on to *very* hot plates.

If you are cooking directly over a flame and not in a double boiler, the flame must be moderately low.

Mistakes in making scrambled eggs are the use of too much butter in the pan, too long cooking of the eggs so that they become leathery, and the introduction of milk, water, bread and so on – which is fatal.

The egg should set slowly – it will remain almost liquid for some time. But when once it has begun to set it is quickly finished and needs constant watching.

RECIPE 5.
American Tea Biscuits.

These delicious little rolls, or scones (the American word 'biscuit' has no exact counterpart in this country) are an excellent substitute for bread at breakfast, tea or supper, and they are very easily and quickly made.

Mix two large teaspoonfuls of baking powder with four cups of sifted flour and one half-teaspoonful of salt. Rub in one large tablespoonful of shortening (butter or lard, or a mixture of half of each) and wet with enough milk to make a soft dough. Handle as little as possible and roll about one inch thick. Cut into squares about two inches across and set these not too close together on a greased baking-sheet. Bake for about twenty minutes in a quick over

In tardy repentance for the lack of exotic novelties
in this book the authors present, for the first time, a

SPECIAL RECIPE

(Courtesy of F. A. M., Esq.)

For one man, one pint of locusts.

Place in the sun in open vessel. Leave for three
days.

Remove head, wings and legs.

Pound well, and boil slowly in plenty of milk,
stirring vigorously, add salt (if available) to
taste, and serve hot when you can wait no
longer.

N.B. – This dish is no good when the breeding
season is well advanced, as the excitable locust is
then little more than skin. Season to be determined
by observation.

This is a genuine East African dish.

SEVEN DINNERS FOR SPRING

		PAGE
I.	Lamb Cutlets Maintenon New Potatoes Young Carrots Mousse of Chocolate	42
II.	Escalopes of Veal with Vegetables Browned Potato Purée Lemon Pie	50
III.	Spring Chicken with Watercress Grilled Tomatoes Sauté Potatoes Rhubarb Princess	61
IV.	Chicken Caroline Spaghetti Peas à la Française Floating Island	71
V.	Lancashire Hotpot Red Cabbage Petits Pots de Crème	82
VI.	Savoury Pork Chops Apple Sauce Braised Seakale Mashed Potatoes Apricot Purée	91
VII. (Fish)	Watercress Soup Baked Lemon Sole Italian Rice Golden Pudding	98

SEVEN DINNERS FOR SUMMER

		PAGE
I.	Veal Emma Braised Cabbage Scalloped Potatoes Iced Gooseberry Fool Cat's Tongue Biscuits	104
II.	Guinea-Fowl à la Mère Doub Golden Potatoes Peas Plum Meringue	111
III.	Spinach Soup Ham and Steak Roll (Cold) Mayonnaise of Broad Beans Soufflé of Potatoes Rothe Grütze	121
IV.	Baked Ham Broad Beans New Potatoes Strawberry Shortcake	133
V.	Veal Chops Rissolé Potatoes (Cooked in Butter) Carrots à la Vichy Globe Artichokes Cream Tarts	141
VI.	Grilled Lamb Cutlets Mint Sauce (Optional) Devonshire Fried Potatoes Runner Beans Milky Rice Pudding with Cherries	151
VII. (Fish)	Salmon Soufflé Garden Peas New Potatoes Hearts of Lettuce Salad Red Currant Fool and Shortbread Fingers	160

SEVEN DINNERS FOR AUTUMN

PAGE

I. Squab Pie   168
    Corn on the Cob
    Baked Pears

II. Chicken Baked in Milk   175
    Braised Celery
    Cheese Potatoes
    Sunshine Cream

III. Poacher's Rabbit   185
     Cauliflower Mould
     Autumn Pudding (Blackberry)
     Junket and Cream

IV. Sausage and Kidneys à la Turbigo   194
    Mashed Potatoes
    Savoury Leeks
    Orange Caramel

V. Braised Veal   203
    Potatoes Duchesse
    Stuffed Red Peppers
    Peach Surprise

VI. Jugged Hare and Vegetables   210
    Rice
    Pineapple Cream

VII. (Fish) Fillets of Whiting   218
             Spaghetti Milanaise
             German Chocolate Pudding

SEVEN DINNERS FOR WINTER

PAGE

I.   Spiced Beef and Butter Beans   226
Artichokes and Tomatoes
Angels' Cream

II.   Steak and Kidney Pie   233
Braised Onions
Creamed Potatoes
Hot Fruit Compote

III.   Roast Stuffed Loin of Mutton   244
Roast Potatoes
Creamed Turnips
Cranberry and Apple Snow

IV.   Fillets of Steak Maître d'Hôtel   252
Baked Tomatoes
Brussels Sprouts
Boiled Potatoes
Amy's Crumb Pie

V.   Roast Ribs of Beef   261
Roast Potatoes
Braised Endive
Caramel Custard

VI.   Boeuf à la Bourgeoise   269
Baked Tomatoes
Potatoes Baked in their Jackets
Treacle Tart

VII. (Fish)   Onion Soup   277
Coquilles St. Jacques
Baked Lemon Apples

INDEX TO RECIPES

USED IN 5/ – DINNERS

Soups

Onion soup, 277
Spinach soup, 121
Watercress soup, 98

Fish

Coquilles St. Jacques (Scallops), 278
Lemon sole, baked, 99
Salmon *Soufflé*, 160
Scallops (*Coquilles St. Jacques*), 278
Whiting, fillets of, baked, 218

Meat, Game and Poultry

Beef, roast ribs of, 261
  ,, spiced and stewed with butter beans, 226
  ,, stewed with olives (*bœuf à la Bourgeoise*), 270
Bœuf à la Bourgeoise (beef stewed with olives), 270
Chicken baked in milk, 175
  ,, Caroline (with lemon and mushroom sauce), 71
  ,, spring, grilled, with watercress, 61
Escalopes of veal with vegetables, 50
Guinea-fowl *à la Mère Doub* (stuffed with olives), 111
Ham, baked, 133
  ,, and steak roll (cold), 123
Hare, jugged, and vegetables, 210
Hotpot, Lancashire, 83

Kidneys and sausages *à la Turbigo* (with onion and tomato sauce), 194
Lamb cutlets, grilled, 151
  ,, Maintenon (with onion and cheese sauce), 42
Lancashire hotpot, 83
Mutton, roast stuffed loin of, 244
Poacher's rabbit (in a pie with mushrooms, onions and parsley), 185
Pork chops, savoury, 91
Rabbit, poacher's (in a pie with mushrooms, onions and parsley), 185
Sausages and kidneys *à la Turbigo* (with onion and tomato sauce), 194
Squab Pie (pie containing meat, vegetables and apple), 168
Steak, fillets of, grilled, (with *maître d'hôtel* butter), 252
Steak and ham roll (cold), 123
  ,, and kidney pie, 233
  ,, and vegetable stew (artichokes and tomatoes), 227
Veal, braised with onions, carrots and turnips, 203
  ,, chops, fried, 141
  ,, Emma (cooked in rolls, with onion and cabbage), 104
  ,, escalopes of, with peas and tomatoes, 50

301

INDEX

Vegetables and Salads

Artichokes, globe, boiled with butter sauce, 144
,, stewed with tomatoes, 227
Beans, broad, boiled, 135
,, broad, in mayonnaise (cold), 125
,, butter, stewed with spiced beef, 226
,, runner, boiled, 154
Brussels sprouts, boiled, 255
Cabbage, braised with veal, 104
,, red, cooked in stock, 85
Carrots, young, cooked in butter, 45
,, à la Vichy (cooked in water and butter), 144
Cauliflower mould (with white sauce), 187
Celery, braised, 178
Corn on the cob (sweet corn), 170
Endive, braised, 263
Leeks, savoury (cooked in butter with tomatoes and onion), 197
Lettuce, salad of hearts of, 163
Onions, braised, 238
Peas à la Française (cooked in stock with onions and parsley), 75
,, garden, boiled, 115, 162
Peppers, red, stuffed and baked, 205
Red cabbage, cooked in stock, 85
,, peppers, stuffed and baked, 205
Seakale, braised, 93
Sweet corn (corn on the cob), 170
Tomatoes, baked, 255, 271
,, fried, 52
Tomatoes, grilled, 65
,, stewed with artichokes, 227
Turnips, creamed, 247

Potatoes, Rice and Spaghetti

Potatoes, baked in their jackets, 271
,, boiled, plain, 256
,, browned purée of, 53
,, buttered (rissolé), 143
,, cheese, 179
,, creamed, 238
,, Devonshire fried, 153
,, duchesse, 204
,, golden, 114
,, mashed (purée of), 93, 196
,, new, 44, 136, 162
,, purée of (mashed), 93, 196
,, purée of, browned, 53
,, ,, soufflé, 127
,, rissolé (cooked in butter), 143
,, roast, 244, 261
,, sauté, 65
,, scalloped, 106
Rice, boiled, 212
,, Italian, 100
Spaghetti, boiled, 74
,, Milanaise, 219

Sweets, Puddings, Pastry and Biscuits

Amy's crumb pie, 257
Angels' (banana) cream, 228
Apples, baked (baked lemon apples), 280
,, and cranberry snow, 247
Apricot purée, 94

302

Autumn (blackberry) pudding, 189

Banana (angels') cream, 228

Blackberry (autumn) pudding, 189

Caramel custard, 264

„ of eggs (floating island), 75

„ of oranges (orange caramel), 198

Cherries, stewed, 156

Chocolate mousse (mousse of chocolate), 46

„ pudding, German (German chocolate pudding), 221

Compote of hot fruit (hot fruit compote), 239

Cranberry and apple snow, 247

Cream, angels' (banana), 228

„ lemon (sunshine cream), 180

„ pineapple, 213

Crumb pie (Amy's crumb pie), 257

Custard, caramel, 264

„ boiled (with cream), 77, 221

Floating island (caramel of eggs), 75

Fool, gooseberry, iced, 107

„ red currant, 164

Fruit compote, hot, 239

German chocolate pudding, 221

Golden pudding, 100

Gooseberry fool, iced, 107

Junket and cream, 190

Lemon (sunshine) cream, 180

„ pie, 55

Meringue crust, 116

Mousse of chocolate, 46

Orange caramel, 198

Pastry, short crust, 55, 146, 273

Peach surprise, 206

Pears, baked, 171

Petits pots de crème (Jamaica), 86

Pineapple cream, 213

Plum meringue, 116

Raspberry and red currant mould (*Rothe Grütze*), 128

Red currant fool, 164

Rhubarb princess, 66

Rice pudding, milky, 155

Rothe Grütze (raspberry and red currant mould), 128

Shortbread fingers, 165

Shortcake, strawberry, 136

Short crust pastry, 55, 146, 273

Strawberry shortcake, 136

Sunshine (lemon) cream, 180

Tarts, cream (jam tarts with cream), 146

„ treacle, 272

Gravies, Salad Dressing, Sauces and Stuffings

Gravy, for roast, beef 262

„ chicken, grilled, 63

„ mutton, roast, 246

„ veal chops, fried, 142

„ veal, escalopes of, 54

Salad dressing, French, 164

Sauce, apple, for pork, 92

„ brown, flavoured with lemon (used in braising veal), 204

„ Caroline (mushroom and lemon), 73

„ jam, 207

„ *maître d'hôtel* (and *maître d'hôtel* butter), 254

„ melted butter, 145

„ *milanaise*, 220

„ mint, 152

„ onion and cheese, 43

Sauce, orange, 229
  ,, sour cream, 113
  ,, white (for cauliflower), 187
  ,, ,, (for binding scallops), 279

Sauce, tomato, 194
Stuffing, herb (for mutton), 244
  ,, ,, (for red peppers), 205
  ,, olive, 112

INDEX TO RECIPES FOR IMPROMPTU MEALS

Vegetarian

American tea biscuits, 295
Baked beans and tomatoes, 290
Scrambled eggs, 294

Fish

Fish, creamed, on toast, 292
Lobster with asparagus, 290
Prawns with spaghetti, 289
Salmon with cream sauce and peas, 288
Salmon with tomatoes and pimento, 288
Sardines on toast, 293

Meat and Chicken

Chicken, potatoes and beans, 291
Corn beef hash, 293
Ham, sweet corn and tomatoes, 289
  ,, tomatoes and spinach, 289

Fruit

Fruit with cream, 291
  ,, fool, 291